THE
WOMEN NOVELISTS

BY

R. BRIMLEY JOHNSON

AUTHOR OF
"TALES FROM CHAUCER" "TOWARDS RELIGION"
"TENNYSON AND HIS POETRY"

HASKELL HOUSE PUBLISHERS LTD.
Publishers of Scarce Scholarly Books
NEW YORK, N. Y. 10012
1972

HASKELL HOUSE PUBLISHERS LTD.

Publishers of Scarce Scholarly Books

280 LAFAYETTE STREET

NEW YORK, N. Y. 10012

Library of Congress Cataloging in Publication Data

Johnson, Reginald Brimley, 1867-1932.
    The women novelists.

    1. Women as authors--Great Britain. 2. English
fiction--18th century--History and criticism.
3. English fiction--19th century--History and criticism.
I. Title.
PR115.J6 1972   823'.009   72-3467
ISBN 0-8383-1496-1

Printed in the United States of America

CONTENTS

CONTENTS

THE WOMEN NOVELISTS

INTRODUCTION

ALTHOUGH women wrote novels before Defoe, the father of English fiction, or Richardson, the founder of the modern novel, we cannot detect any peculiarly feminine elements in their work, or profitably consider it apart from the general development of prose.

In the beginning they copied men, and saw through men's eyes, because—here and elsewhere—they assumed that men's dicta and practice in life and art were their only possible guides and examples. Women to-day take up every form of fiction attempted by men, because they assume that their powers are as great, their right to express themselves equally varied.

But there was a period, covering about a hundred years, during which women " found themselves " in fiction, and developed the art, along lines of their own, more or less independently. This century may conveniently be divided into three periods, which it is the object of the following pages to analyse :

From the publication of *Evelina* to the publication of *Sense and Sensibility*, 1778–1811.

From the publication of *Sense and Sensibility* to the publication of *Jane Eyre*, 1811–1847.

From the publication of *Jane Eyre* to the publication of *Daniel Deronda*, 1847–1876.

It may be noticed, however, in passing to the establishment of a feminine school by Fanny Burney, that individual women did pioneer work ; among whom the earliest, and the most important, is "the ingenious Mrs. Aphra Behn" (1640–1689). She is generally believed to have been the first woman " to earn a livelihood in a profession, which, hitherto, had been exclusively monopolized by men,"—" she was, moreover, the first to introduce milk punch into England " ! For much of her work she adopted a masculine pseudonym and, with it, a reckless licence no doubt essential to success under the Restoration. Yet she wrote " the first prose story that can be compared with things that already existed in foreign literatures " ;

and, allowing for a few rather outspoken descriptive passages, there is nothing peculiarly objectionable in her *Oroonoko; or, The History of the Royal Slave.* Making use of her own experience of the West Indies, acquired in childhood, she invented the " noble savage," the " natural man," long afterwards made fashionable by Rousseau ; and boldly contrasted the ingenuous virtues, and honour, of this splendid heathen with Christian treachery and avarice. The "great and just character of Oroonoko," indeed, would scarcely have satisfied " Revolutionary " ideals of the primitive ; since he was inordinately proud of his birth and his beauty, and killed his wife from an "artificial " sense of honour. But there is a naïvely exaggerated simplicity in Mrs. Behn's narrative ; which does faithfully represent, as she herself expresses it, "an absolute idea of the first state of innocence, before man knew how to sin." Whence she declares " it is most evident and plain, that simple nature is the most harmless, inoffensive, and virtuous mistress. It is she alone, if she were permitted, that better instructs the world than all the inventions of man : *religion would here but destroy that tranquility they possess by ignorance ; and laws would but teach them to know offence, of which now they have no notion* . . . they have a native justice, which knows no fraud ; and they understand no vice, or cunning, but when they are taught by the white men."

Our author is quite uncompromising in this matter ; and her eulogy of " fig-leaves " should refute the most cynical : " I have seen a handsome young Indian, dying for love of a beautiful Indian maid ; but all his courtship was, to fold his arms, pursue her with his eyes, and sighs were all his language : while she, as if no such lover were present, or rather as if she desired none such, carefully guarded her eyes from beholding him ; and never approached him, but she looked down with all the blushing modesty I have seen in the most severe and cautious of our world."

The actual story of *Oroonoko* will hardly move us to-day ; and the final scene, where that Prince and gentleman is seen smoking a pipe (!) as the horrid Christians " hack off " his limbs one by one, comes dangerously near the ludicrous. Still we may " hope," with the modest authoress, that " the reputation of her pen is considerable enough to make his glorious name to survive all ages."

It should finally be remarked that Aphra fore-
stalls one more innovation of the next century,
by introducing slight descriptions of scenery; and
that here, as always, she arrested her readers'
attention by plunging straight into the story.

Two other professional women of that generation deserve mention : Mrs. Manley (1672–1724),
author of the scurrilous *New Atalantis*, and Mrs.
Heywood (or Haywood) (1693–1756), editor of
the *Female Spectator*. Both were employed by their
betters for the secret promotion of vile libels—
the former political, the latter literary ; and both
wrote novels of some vigour, but deservedly forgotten : although the latest, and best, of Mrs.
Manley's were written after *Pamela*, and bear
striking witness to the influence of Richardson.

A few more years bring us to the true birth of the
modern novel ; when Sarah Fielding (1710–1768),
whose *David Simple*, in an unfortunate attempt
to combine sentiment with the picaresque, revealed some of her brother's humour and the
decided influence of Richardson. And though
The Female Quixote of Charlotte Lennox
(1720–1804) has been pronounced " more absurd
than any of the romances which it was designed

to ridicule," Macaulay himself allows it "great merit, when considered as a wild satirical harlequinade"; and it remains an early, if not the first, example of conscious revolt against the artificial tyrannies of " Romance," of which the evil influences on the art of fiction were soon to be triumphantly abolished for ever by a sister-authoress.

THE FIRST WOMAN NOVELIST

(Fanny Burney, 1752–1840)

It is, to-day, a commonplace of criticism that the novel proper, though partially forestalled in subject and treatment by Defoe, began with Richardson's *Pamela* in 1740. The main qualities which distinguish this work from our earlier "romances" were the attempt to copy, or reproduce, real life; and the choice of middle-class society for dramatis personæ. It is difficult for us to realise how long the prejudice against "middle-class" characters held sway; but no doubt Christopher North reflected the sentiments of the majority in 1829 when he represented the "Shepherd" declaring it to be his "profound conviction that the strength o' human nature lies either in the highest or lowest estate of life. Characters in books should either be kings, and princes, and nobles, and on a level with them, like heroes; or peasants, shepherds, farmers, and the like, includin' a' orders amaist o' our ain working population. The intermediate

class—that is, leddies and gentlemen in general
—are no worth the Muse's while ; for their life
is made up chiefly o' mainners,—mainners,—
mainners ;—you canna see the human creters for
their claes ; and should ane o' them commit
suicide in despair, in lookin' on the dead body,
you are mair taen up wi' its dress than its de-
cease." The " romance " only condescended below
Prince or Peer for the exhibition of the Criminal.
It aimed at exaggeration in every detail for
dramatic effect. It recognised no limit to the
resources of wealth, the beauty of virtue, the
splendour of heroism, or the corruption of villainy.
It permitted the supernatural. Fielding clearly
considers it necessary to apologise for the *vulgarity*
of mere " human nature " :

" The provision, then, which we have here made, is
no other than Human Nature : nor do I fear that any
sensible reader, though most luxurious in his taste, will
start, cavil, or be offended because I have named but
one article. The tortoise, as the alderman of Bristol,
well learned in eating, knows by much experience, besides
the delicious calipash and calipee, contains many different
kinds of food ; nor can the learned reader be ignorant,
that in human nature, though here collected under one
general name, is such prodigious variety, that a cook will
have sooner gone through all the several species of animal

and vegetable food in the world, than an author will be able to exhaust so extensive a subject.

" An objection may perhaps be apprehended from the more delicate, that this dish is too vulgar and common ; for what else is the subject of all the romances, novels, plays, and poems, with which the stalls abound ? Many exquisite viands might be rejected by the epicure, if it was sufficient cause for his contemning of them as common and vulgar, that something was to be found in the most paltry alleys under the same name. In reality, true nature is as difficult to be met with in authors, as the Bayonne ham, or Bologna sausage, is to be found in the shops.

" But the whole, to continue the metaphor, consists in the cooking of the author ; for, as Mr. Pope tells us,—

> ' True wit is nature to advantage dress'd ;
> What oft was thought, but ne'er so well express'd.'

" The same animal which hath the honour to have some part of his flesh eaten at the table of a duke, may perhaps be degraded in another part, and some of his limbs gibbetted, as it were, in the vilest stall in town. Where then lies the difference between the food of the nobleman and the porter, if both are at dinner on the same ox or calf, but in the seasoning, the dressing, the garnishing, and the setting forth ? Hence the one provokes and incites the most languid appetite, and the other turns and palls that which is the sharpest and keenest.

" In like manner the excellence of the mental entertainment consists less in the subject than in the author's skill in well dressing it up. How pleased, therefore, will the reader be to find that we have, in the following

work, adhered closely to one of the highest principles
of the best cook which the present age, or perhaps that
of Heliogabalus, hath produced ? This great man, as
is well known to all lovers of polite eating, begins at
first by setting plain things before his hungry guests,
rising afterwards by degrees, as their stomachs may be
supposed to decrease, to the very quintessence of sauce
and spices.

" In like manner we shall represent human nature
at first, to the keen appetite of our reader, in that more
plain and simple manner in which it is found in the
country, and shall hereafter hash and ragout it with all
the high French and Italian seasoning of affectation
and vice which courts and cities afford. By these means,
we doubt not but our reader may be rendered desirous
to read on for ever, as the great person just above mentioned, is supposed to have made some persons eat."

Samuel   Richardson,   printer,   revolutionised
fiction.   He   inaugurated   a   method   of   novel-
writing :   shrewdly   adapted,   and   developed,   by
Fielding ;   boisterously   copied   by   Smollett ;
humorously   varied   by   Goldsmith   and   Sterne.
And   when   the   new   ideal   of   realism   and   simple
narrative   had   been   thus,   more   or   less   consciously,
established   as   fit   fruit   for   the   circulating   library :
that " evergreen   tree   of   diabolical   knowledge,"
finally   purified   of   all   offence   against   decency,
was   planted   in   every   household   by   a   timid   and

bashful young lady, who "hemmed and stitched from breakfast to dinner with scrupulous regularity."

The mental development of Frances Burney, authoress of *Evelina*, was encouraged by "no governess, no teacher of any art or of any language." Her father's library contained only *one novel*; and she does not appear to have supplemented it in this particular. But the peculiar circumstances of Dr. Burney's social position, and the infectious enthusiasm of his artistic temperament, provided his daughter with very exceptional opportunities for the study of material appropriate to the construction of a modern novel. On the one hand, he permitted her free intercourse "with those whom butlers and waiting-maids call vulgar"; and, on the other, he gave her every opportunity of watching Society at ease in the company of artists and men of letters. At his concerts and tea-parties, again, she often saw Johnson and Garrick; Bruce, Omai, and the "lions" of her generation; the peers and the politicians; the ambassadors and the travellers; the singers and the fiddlers.

And, finally, if her most worthy stepmother

has been derided for the conventionality which discouraged the youthful " observer," and dictated a " bonfire " for her early manuscripts, it may not be altogether fanciful to conjecture that the domestic ideals of feminine propriety thus inculcated had some hand in shaping the precise direction of the influence which Fanny was destined to exert upon the development of her art.

For if *Evelina* was modelled on the work of Richardson, and the fathers of fiction, who had so recently passed away, it nevertheless inaugurated a new departure—the expression of a feminine outlook on life. It was, frankly and obviously, written by a woman for women, though it captivated men of the highest intellect.

We need not suppose that Johnson's pet " character-monger " set out with any intention of accomplishing this reform ; but the woman's view is so obvious on every page that we can scarcely credit the general assumption of " experienced " *masculine* authorship, which was certainly prevalent during the few weeks it remained anonymous. It would have been far more reasonable for the public to have accepted the legend of its being written by a girl of seventeen. For the heroine is represented as being no older; and though Miss Burney was twenty-six at the time, she has been most extraordinarily successful in assuming the tone of extreme youth, and thus emphasising still further the innovation. Its main subject is "The Introduction of a Young Lady to the World"; and being told in letters from the heroine to her guardian, could scarcely have been better arranged, by a self-conscious artist, for the exposition of the novelty. On the other hand, the success of its execution doubtless owes much to the author's spontaneity and to her untrained mind. It would seem that she was blissfully unconscious of any accepted "rules" in composition; and even in *Cecilia*, generally supposed to be partially disfigured by Johnson's advice, it is only in the structure of her sentences that she attempted to be "correct." It is a more complex variant of the same theme, with a precisely similar inspiration : the manipulation of her own experience of life, and her own comments thereon.

It is obvious that we can only realise the precise nature of what she accomplished for fiction by comparing her work with Richardson's, since Fielding, Smollett, and Sterne wove all their stories

about a " hero," and even Goldsmith drew women
through the spectacles of a naïvely " superior "
and obviously masculine vicar. Richardson, on
the other hand, was admittedly an expert in the
analysis of the feminine. We must recognise a
lack of virility in touch and outlook. The prim
exactitude of his cautious realism, however startling
in comparison with anything before *Pamela*, has
much affinity with what our ancestors might have
expected from their womenkind. Yet his women
are quite obviously studies, not self-revelations.
We can fancy that Pamela sat on his knee to have
her portrait taken ; while he was giving such infinite
care to Clarissa's drapery on the model's throne.
We can only marvel that he could ever determine
whether Clementina or Miss Harriet Byron were
a more worthy mate for " the perfect man."
Verily they were all as men made them ; exquisite
creatures, born for our delight, but regulated
by our taste in loveliness and virtue. That mar-
marvellous little eighteenth - century tradesman
understood their weaknesses no less than their
perfections ; but the fine lines of his brush show
through every word or expression : the delicacy
of outline is deliberately obtained by art. They

are patently the fruits of acute observation, keen sympathy, and subtle draughtsmanship. They remain lay figures, posed for the centre of the picture. The showman is there, pulling the strings. And above all they are man-made. For all his extraordinary insight Richardson can only see woman from the outside. Our *consciousness* of his skill proves it is conscious. His world still centres round the hero : the rustic fine gentleman, the courtly libertine, or the immaculate male.

Fanny Burney reverses the whole process. To begin with external evidence : it is Evelina who tells the tale, and every person or incident is regarded from her point of view. The resultant difference goes to the heart of the matter. The reader does not here feel that he is studying a new type of female : he is making a new friend. Evelina and Cecilia speak for themselves throughout. There is no sense of effort or study ; not because Fanny Burney is a greater artist or has greater power to conceal her art, but because, for the accomplishment . of her task, she has simply to be herself. It is here, in fact, that we find the peculiar charm, and the supreme achievement, of the women who founded the school. By never

attempting professional study of life outside their
own experience, they were enabled to produce a
series of feminine " Confessions " ; which remain
almost unique as human documents. We must
recognise that it was Richardson who had made
this permissible. He broke away, for ever, from
the extravagant impossibilities and unrealities of
Romance. He copied life, and life moreover in
its prosaic aspect—the work-a-day, unpicturesque
experience of the middle-class. But still he
lingered among its crises. It is not that in
his days men were still given to the expression
of emotion by words, and deeds, of violence. While
beautiful maidens were liable to be driven furiously
by the villain into the presence of an unfrocked
clergyman ; while money could buy a whole
army of accomplices for their undoing ; Richardson
remains a realist in the narration of such episodes.
We are here referring to the fact that his stories
are all concerned with the elaborate development
of one central emotion or the analysis of one pre-
dominating character. They are pictures of life
composed for the exhibition of a slightly pheno-
menal aspect : the depths of human nature, not
commonly obvious to us in the moods of a day.

It was reserved for Fanny Burney, and still more Jane Austen, to " make a story " out of the trivialities of our everyday existence ; to reveal humanity at a tea-party or an afternoon call. This is, of course, but carrying on his reform one step further. The women, besides introducing the new element of their own especial point of view, made the new realism strictly *domestic* ; and learned to depend, even less than he, upon the exceptional, more obviously dramatic, or less normal, incidents of actual life. If Richardson invented the ideal of fidelity to human nature, Miss Burney selected its everyday habits and costume for imitation. Evelina's account of " shopping " in London would not fit into Richardson's scheme ; while the many incidents and characters, introduced merely for comic effect, lie outside his province.

Miss Burney's ideal for heroines, indeed, must seem singularly old-fashioned to-day ; nor do we delight in *Evelina* for those passages to which its author devoted her most serious ambitions. She does not excel in minute, or sustained, characterisation ; nor have we ever entirely confirmed the appreciation which declares that her work was

" inspired by one consistent vein of passion, never relaxed." The passion of Evelina—by which, however, the critic does *not* mean her love for Orville—has always seemed to us melodramatic and artificial. We have little, or no, patience with those refined tremors and heart-burnings which completely prostrate the young lady at the mere possibility of seeing her long-lost father. It is not in human nature to feel so deeply about anyone we have never seen, of whom we know nothing but evil.

No blame attaches to Miss Burney as an artist in this respect, however, because she was intent upon the revelation of *sensibility*, that most elusive of female graces on which our grandmothers were wont to pride themselves. Any definition of this quality, suited to our comprehension to-day, would seem beyond the subtleties of emotional analysis ; but we may observe, as some indication of its meaning, that no *man* was ever supposed, or expected, to possess it. Sensibility, in fact, was the acknowledged privilege of *ladies*—as distinguished at once from gentlemen or women ; particularly becoming in youth ; and indicating the well-bred, the elegant, and the fastidious.

It must not, of course, be confounded with " susceptibility," a sign of weakness ; for though it,
temporarily, unfitted the lady for action or speech,
it was the expression of deep, permanent, feeling
and of exquisite taste. Her gentle voice rendered
inaudible by tears, her streaming eyes buried in
the cushions of her best sofa, or on the bosom of
her best friend, the beautiful maiden would fondly
persuade herself that her life was blighted for ever-
more. Pierced to the heart by a cold world, a
faithless friend, or a stern parent, as the case might
be, she would terrify those who loved her by the
wild expression of her eyes, the dead whiteness of
her lips, her feeble gesticulations, and the disorder
of her whole person. In the end, mercifully, she
would—faint ! Under such influences, we cannot
distinguish very explicitly between the effects of
joy or sorrow. Evelina is scarcely more natural
about her transports at discovering a brother,
or in the final *satisfaction* of her filial instincts,
than in her alarm about " how He would receive
her," already mentioned.

We are not justified, on the other hand, in
supposing that a heroine should only exhibit sensibility on some real emotional catastrophe. There

was a tendency, we have observed, in "elegant females" to be utterly abashed and penetrated with remorse, covered with shame, trembling with alarm, and on the verge of hysterics—from joy or grief—upon most trivial provocation. A tone, a look, even a movement, if unexpected or mysterious, was generally sufficient to upset the nice adjustment of their mental equilibrium. "Have I done wrong? Am I misunderstood? Is it possible he *really* loves me?" The dear creatures passed through life on the edge of a precipice : on the borderland between content, despair, and the seventh heaven.

The wonder of it all comes from admitting that Miss Burney actually reconciles us to such absurdities. Except in the passionate scenes, Evelina's sensibility is one of her chief charms. In some mysterious and subtle fashion, it really indicates the superiority of her mind and her essential refinement. She will be prattling away, with all the naïveté of genuine innocence, about her delight in the condescending perfections of the "noble Orville," and then—at *one* word of warning from her beloved guardian — the whole world assumes other aspects, no man may be trusted, and she would fly at once to peace, and forgetfulness, in the country. We smile, inevitably, at the " complete *ingénue* " ; but the quick response to her old friend's loving anxiety, the transparent candour of a purity which, if instinctive, is not dependent on ignorance, combine to form a really " engaging " personality.

It may be that we have here discovered the secret of sensibility—a perception of the fine shades, and instant responsiveness to them. There is, however, a most instructive passage in *The Mysteries of Udolpho* which throws much light on this matter. Mrs. Radcliffe has every claim to be heard, for her heroines are much addicted to sensibility. The passage occurs in an early chapter ; when St. Aubert is dying, and naturally wishes to impress upon his orphan daughter such truths as may guide her safely through life. It has, therefore, all the significance of the death-bed ; while he " had never thought more justly, or expressed himself more clearly, than he did now." Under such circumstances, and in such manner, did that worthy gentleman discourse on

The Dangers of Sensibility

" Above all, my dear Emily, said he, do not indulge in the pride of fine feeling, the romantic error of amiable minds. Those who really possess sensibility ought early to be taught that it is a dangerous quality, which is continually extracting the excess of misery or delight from every surrounding circumstance. And since, in our passage through this world, painful circumstances occur more frequently than pleasing ones, and since our sense of evil is, I fear, more acute than our sense of good, we become the victim of our feelings, unless we can in some degree command them. I know you will say—for you are young, my Emily—I know you will say, that you are contented sometimes to suffer, rather than give up your refined sense of happiness at others ; but when your mind has been long harassed by vicissitude, you will be content to rest, and you will then recover from your delusion : you will perceive that the phantom of happiness is exchanged for the substance ; for happiness arises in a state of peace, not of tumult : it is of a temperate and uniform nature ; and can no more exist in a heart that is continually alive to minute circumstances than in one that is dead to feeling. You see, my dear, that, though I would guard you against the dangers of sensibility, I am not an advocate for apathy. At your age, I should have said *that* is a vice more hateful than all the errors of sensibility, and I say so still. I call it a *vice*, because it leads to positive evil. In this, however, it does no more than an ill-governed sensibility, which, by such a rule, might also be called a vice ; but the evil of the former is of more general consequence. . . .

" I would not teach you to become insensible, if I could
—I would only warn you of the evils of susceptibility,
and point out how you may avoid them. Beware, my
love, I conjure you, of that self-delusion which has been
fatal to the peace of many persons—beware of priding
yourself on the gracefulness of sensibility : if you yield
to this vanity, your happiness is lost for ever. Always
remember how much more valuable is the strength of
fortitude, than the grace of sensibility. Do not, however, confound fortitude with apathy : apathy cannot
know the virtue. Remember, too, that one act of bene-
ficence, one act of real usefulness, is worth all the abstract
sentiment in the world. Sentiment is a disgrace, instead
of an ornament, unless it lead us to good actions : the
miser, who thinks himself respectable merely because
he possesses wealth, and thus mistakes the means of
doing good for the actual accomplishment of it, is not
more blameable than the man of sentiment without
active virtue. You may have observed persons, who
delight so much in this sort of sensibility to sentiment,
that they turn from the distressed, and because their
sufferings are painful to be contemplated, do not
endeavour to relieve them. How despicable is that
humanity which can be contented to pity where it might
assuage ! "

And we are finally disposed to question whether
Miss Burney herself were actually conscious of the
subtlety with which she has allowed her heroine
to reveal, in every sentence, the scarcely perceptible
advance of her unsuspected " partiality." The

reader, of course, recognises Orville at sight for what he proves to be in the final event; but he frequently reminds us of Sir Charles Grandison—and in nothing so much, perhaps, as in his gentlemanly precautions against letting himself go or expressing his emotions. Only a woman of real delicacy, indeed, could have imagined, or appreciated, the self-effacement with which he helps and protects the guileless heroine from her unprincipled admirers; and it required genuine refinement to give him the courage evinced by his tactful inquiries into her circumstances and his most fatherly advice. The whole development of the relations between them must be acknowledged as a triumph of art, and conclusive evidence of " nice " feeling.

It is impossible, I think, to put Cecilia herself on a level with Evelina; though I personally have always felt that the more crowded canvas of the *book* so entitled, and its greater variety of incident, reveal more mature power. But it is less spontaneous and, in a certain sense, less original. To begin with, Cecilia is always conscious of her superiority. Like her sister heroine, a country " miss," and suddenly tossed into Society without any proper guidance, she yet assumes the centre of the stage without effort, and queens it over the most experienced, by virtue of beauty and wealth. It may be doubted if she has much " sensibility " for everyday matters : whereas the lavish expenditure of emotional fireworks over the haughty Delviles, and the melodramatic sufferings they entail, are most intolerably protracted, and entirely destroy our interest in the conclusion of the narrative. The occasional scene, or episode, we complained of in *Evelina,* is here extended to long chapters, or books, of equally strained passion on a more complex issue. Fortunately they all come at the end, and need not disturb our enjoyment of the main story ; though, indeed, the whole plot depends far more on melodramatic effect. Mr. Harrell's abominable recklessness, and his sensational suicide, the criminal passion of Mr. Monckton, and the story of Henrietta Belfield, carry us into depths beyond the reach of *Evelina,* where Miss Burney herself does not walk with perfect safety. And, in our judgment, such experiences diminish the charm of her heroine.

Yet in the main Cecilia possesses, and exhibits those primarily feminine qualities which now made their first appearance in English fiction, being beyond man's power to delineate. She, too, is that " Womanly Woman " whom Mr. Bernard Shaw has so eloquently denounced. She has the magnetic power of personal attraction ; the charm of mystery ; the strength of weakness ; the irresistible appeal with which Nature has endowed her for its own purposes : so seldom present in the man-made heroine, certainly not revealed to Samuel Richardson and his great contemporaries.

For the illustration of our main theme, we have so far dwelt upon the revelation of womanhood achieved by Miss Burney. It is time to consider, in more detail, her application of the new " realism," her method of " drawing from life," now first recognised as the proper function of the novelist. It is here that her unique education, or experience, has full play. Instead of depending, like Richardson, upon the finished analysis of a few characters, centred about one emotional situation, or of securing variety of interests and character-types, *à la* Fielding, by use of the " wild-oats " convention, she works up the astonishing " contrasts " in life, which she had herself been privileged to witness, and achieves comedy by the abnormal mixture of Society. Thus she is able to find drama in domesticity. Her most original effects are produced in the drawing-room or the assembly, at a ball or a theatre, in the "long walks" of Vauxhall or Ranelagh : wherever, and whenever, mankind is seen only at surface-value, enjoying the pleasures and perils of everyday existence. How vividly, as Macaulay remarks, did she conjecture "the various scenes, tragic and comic, through which the poor motherless girl, highly connected on one side, meanly connected on the other, might have to pass. A crowd of unreal beings, good and bad, grave and ludicrous, surrounded the pretty, timid young orphan : a coarse sea-captain ; an ugly insolent fop, blazing in a superb court-dress ; another fop, as ugly and as insolent, but lodged on Snow Hill, and tricked out in second-hand finery for the Hampstead ball ; an old woman, all wrinkles and rouge, flirting her fan with the air of a Miss of seventeen, and screaming in a dialect made up of vulgar French and vulgar English ; a poet lean and ragged, with a broad Scotch accent. By degrees these shadows acquired stronger and stronger consistence : the impulse which urged Fanny to write became irresistible; and the result was the history of Evelina."

Of what must seem, to our thinking, the extraordinary licence permitted to persons accounted gentlemen, Miss Burney avails herself to the utmost; and Evelina is scarcely less often embarrassed or distressed by Willoughby's violence and the insolence of Lord Merton, than by the stupid vulgarity of the Branghtons and " Beau " Smith. We have primarily the sharp contrast between Society and Commerce—each with its own standards of comfort, pleasure, and decorum; and secondarily, a great variety of individual character (and ideal) within both groups. The " contrasts " of Cecilia are, in the main, more specifically individual, lacking the one general sharp class division, and may be more accurately divided into one group of Society " types," another of Passions exemplified in persons obsessed by a single idea. It is " in truth a grand and various picture-gallery, which presented to the eye a long series of men and women, each marked by some strong peculiar feature. There were avarice and prodigality, the pride of blood and the pride of money, morbid restlessness and morbid apathy

frivolous garrulity, supercilious silence, a Demo-
critus to laugh at everything, and a Heraclitus to
lament over everything. . . . Mr. Delvile never
opens his lips without some allusion to his own
birth and station ; or Mr. Briggs, without some
allusion to the hoarding of money ; or Mr. Hobson,
without betraying the self-indulgence and self-
importance of a purse-proud upstart ; or Mr.
Simkins, without uttering some sneaking remark
for the purpose of currying favour with his cus-
tomers ; or Mr. Meadows, without expressing
apathy and weariness of life ; or Mr. Albany,
without declaiming about the vices of the rich
and the miseries of the poor ; or Mrs. Belfield,
without some indelicate eulogy on her son ; or
Lady Margaret, without indicating jealousy of her
husband. Morrice is all skipping, officious impertinence, Mr. Gosport all sarcasm, Lady Honoria all
lively prattle, Miss Larolles all silly prattle."

It is primarily, indeed, a most diverting picture
of manners ; and if, as we have endeavoured to
show, Miss Burney advanced on Richardson by
the revelation of womanhood in her heroines, the
realism of her minor persons must be applauded
rather for its variety in outward seeming than for

its subtlety of characterisation. As Ben Jonson
hath it :

> " When some one peculiar quality
> Does so possess a man, that it doth draw
> All his effects, his spirits, and his powers,
> In their confluxions all to run one way,
> This may be truly said to be a *humour*."

It is in the exhibition of " humours " that our
authoress delights and excels.

Of any particular construction Miss Burney
was entirely guiltless ; in this respect, of course,
lagging far behind Fielding. She has no style,
beyond a most attractive spontaneity ; writing in
" true *woman's* English, clear, natural, and lively."
Under the watchful eye of Dr. Johnson, indeed,
she made some attempt at the rounded period,
the " elegant " antithesis, in *Cecilia* : but, regretting
the obvious effort, we turn here again, with re-
newed delight, to the flowing simplicity of her
dramatic dialogue.

There is no occasion, at this time of day, to dwell
upon her sparkling wit, though we may note in
passing its obviously feminine inspiration—as
opposed to the more scholarly subtleties of Fielding—and its patent superiority to, for example,

the kitten-sprightliness of Richardson's "Lady G." We cannot claim that Miss Burney made any particular *advance* in this matter ; but, here again, her work stands out as the first permanent expression—at least in English—of that shrewd vivacity and quickness of observation with which so many a woman, who might have founded a salon, has been wont to enliven the conversation of the home and to promote the gaiety of social gatherings. We must recognise, on the other hand, that, if commonly more refined than her generation, Miss Burney has yielded to its prejudice against foreigners in some coarseness towards Madame Duval ; as we marvel at her father's approval of this detail—while actually deploring the vigour of her contempt for Lovel, the fop !

Finally, for all technicalities of her art, Miss Burney remains an amateur in authorship, who, by a lucky combination of genius and experience, was destined to utter the first word for women in the most popular form of literature ; and to point the way to her most illustrious successors for the perfection of the domestic novel.

Probably the most important, more or less contemporary, criticism on the early achievements of women, was uttered—incidentally—by Hazlitt in 1818. Dismissing Miss Edgeworth's *Tales* as " a kind of pedantic, pragmatical common-sense, tinctured with the pertness and pretensions of the paradoxes to which they are so complacently opposed," assigning the first place to Mrs. Radcliffe for her power of " describing the indefinable and embodying a phantom," he says of Miss Burney and of feminine work generally :

" Madame D'Arblay is a mere common observer of manners, *and also a very woman.* It is this last circumstance which forms the peculiarity of her writings, and distinguishes them from those masterpieces [1] which I have before mentioned. She is a quick, lively, and accurate observer of persons and things ; but she always looks at them with a consciousness of her sex, and in that point of view in which it is the particular business and interest of women to observe them . . . her *forte* is in describing the absurdities and affectations of external behaviour, or the manners of people in company. . . . The form such characters or people might be supposed to assume for a night at a masquerade. . . .

" Women, in general, have a quicker perception of any oddity or singularity of character than men, and are more alive to any absurdity which arises from a violation of the rules of society, or a deviation from established custom. This partly arises from the restraints on their

---

[1] Of Richardson, Fielding, etc.

own behaviour, which turn their attention constantly
on the subject, and partly from other causes. The surface
of their minds, like that of their bodies, seems of a finer
texture than ours; more soft, and susceptible of immediate
impulses. They have less muscular strength, less power
of continued voluntary attention, of reason, passion,
and imagination ; but they are more easily impressed
with whatever appeals to their senses or habitual pre-
judices. The intuitive perception of their minds is less
disturbed by any abstruse reasonings on causes or consequences. They learn the idiom of character, as they
acquire that of language, by rote, without troubling themselves about the principles. Their observation is not the
less accurate on that account, as far as it goes, for it has
been well said that ' there is nothing so true as habit.'

" There is little other power in Madame D'Arblay's
novels than that of immediate observation ; her characters, whether of refinement or vulgarity, are equally
superficial and confined. The whole is a question of form,
whether that form is adhered to or infringed. It is this
circumstance which takes away dignity and interest from
her story and sentiments, and makes the one so teasing
and tedious, and the other so insipid. The difficulties
in which she involves her heroines are too much ' Female
Difficulties ' ; they are difficulties created out of nothing.
The author appears to have no other idea of refinement
than that it is the reverse of vulgarity ; but the reverse
of vulgarity is fastidiousness and affectation. There is a
true and a false delicacy. Because a vulgar country Miss
would answer ' Yes ' to a proposal of marriage in the
first page, Madame D'Arblay makes it a proof of an excess

of refinement, and an indispensable point of etiquette in
her young ladies, to postpone the answer to the end of
five volumes, without the smallest reason for their doing so,
and with every reason to the contrary. . . . The whole
artifice of her fable consists in coming to no conclusion.
Her ladies ' stand so upon their going,' that they do not
go at all. . . . They would consider it as quite indecorous
to run downstairs though the house were in flames, or to
move an inch off the pavement though a scaffolding was
falling. She has formed to herself an abstract idea of
perfection in common behaviour, which is quite as
romantic and impracticable as any other idea of the
sort. . . . Madame D'Arblay has woven a web of difficulties for her heroines, something like the great silken
threads in which the shepherdesses entangled the steed
of Cervantes' hero, who swore, in his fine enthusiastic way,
that he would sooner cut his passage to another world
than disturb the least of these beautiful meshes."

The critic recognises the essential quality of
Miss Burney's work—its femininity—which he
reckons, curiously enough, as a fault. But pre-
judices die hard, and it is evident that he is not
ready for the new point of view.

Evelina, 1778.
Cecilia, 1782.
Camilla, 1796.
The Wanderer, 1814.

A PICTURE OF YOUTH

It is natural, if not inevitable, that the later works of Miss Burney should have been suffered to remain unread and unremembered. Critics have told us that they only face them unwillingly, from a sense of duty; and none has ventured a second time. To-day, no doubt, readers would hesitate before the five, or more, volumes of extenuated sensibility.

And yet, though we should not ask for any reversal of this verdict, there are points of interest —at any rate in *Camilla*—which will repay attention. The fact is, that in this work Miss Burney has given full rein to her ideal of women, her conception of home life, and her notions about marriage : all eminently characteristic of the age, and full of suggestion as to the work of women.

We have again, as the closing paragraph reminds us, "a picture of youth," primarily feminine ; but Camilla is no mere repetition either of Evelina or Cecilia. She has even more sensibility, and a new quality of most attractive impulsiveness, which is perpetually leading her into difficulties.

There is a double contrast, or comparison, of types. The heroine's uncle—Sir Hugh Tyrold—seems to have been conceived as a parody of the young lady herself. He flies off at a tangent—far more youthfully than she—changes his will three or four times in the first few chapters, and is constantly upsetting the whole family by most ridiculous " plans " for their happiness.

On the other hand, Edgar Mandlebert—the hero —suffers from too much caution; implanted, it is true, by his worthy tutor ; but obviously " at home " in his nature. Practically the whole five volumes are concerned with the misunderstandings produced by Camilla's hasty self-sacrifices, and his care in studying her character, without the key to her motives. It would be easy, indeed, to describe the plot as a prolonged " much ado about nothing." The sentiments involved are palpably strained, absurdly high-flown, and singularly unbalanced. But we should remember two reasons for modifying our judgment, and hesitating before a complete condemnation.

In the first place, the ideals for women, and for all intercourse between the sexes, differ in nearly every particular from those of our own

day ; and, in the second, these people were
almost ridiculously young. Love affairs, and often
marriage, began for them when they were fifteen ;
and it may be that were our own sons and daughters
put to the test at that age, their deeds and sentiments might surprise us considerably.

" In the bosom of her respectable family resided Camilla.
Nature, with a bounty the most profuse, had been lavish
to her of attractions ; Fortune, with a moderation yet
kinder, had placed her between luxury and indigence.
Her abode was in the parsonage-house of Etherington,
beautifully situated in the unequal county of Hampshire,
and in the vicinity of the varied landscapes of the New
Forest. Her father, the rector, was the younger son of
the house of Tyrold. The living, though not considerable, enabled its incumbent to attain every rational
object of his modest and circumscribed wishes ; to bestow
upon a deserving wife whatever her own forbearance
declined not ; to educate a lovely race of one son and
three daughters, with that expansive propriety, which
unites improvement for the future with present enjoyment.
     " In goodness of heart, and in principles of piety, this
exemplary couple were bound to each other by the most
perfect union of character, though in their tempers there
was a contrast which had scarce the gradation of a single
shade to smooth off its abrupt dissimilitude. Mr. Tyrold,
gentle with wisdom, and benign in virtue, saw with com-
passion all imperfections but his own, and there doubled
the severity which to others he spared. Yet the mild-

ness that urged him to pity blinded him not to approve ;
his equity was unerring, though his judgment was in-
dulgent. His partner had a firmness of mind which
nothing could shake : calamity found her resolute ;
even prosperity was powerless to lull her duties asleep.
The exalted character of her husband was the pride of
her existence, and the source of her happiness. He was
not merely her standard of excellence, but of endurance,
since her sense of his worth was the criterion for her
opinion of all others. This instigated a spirit of comparison, which is almost always uncandid, and which here could
rarely escape proving injurious. Such, at its very best,
is the unskilfulness of our fallible nature, that even the
noble principle which impels our love of right, misleads
us but into new deviations, when its ambition presumes
to point at perfection. In this instance, however, dis-
tinctness of disposition stifled not reciprocity of affection—that magnetic concentration of all marriage felicity ;
—Mr. Tyrold revered while he softened the rigid virtues
of his wife, who adored while she fortified the melting
humanity of her husband."

Mrs. Tyrold, in fact, was a most alarming lady ;
and as that " sad fellow," their son Lionel—one
of " the merry blades of Oxford "—remarked with
spirit, " A good father is a very serious misfortune
to a poor lad like me, as the world runs ; it causes
one such confounded gripes of conscience for every
little awkward thing one does."

It will be seen, at once, that such surroundings

promised that " repose " so " welcome to the
worn and to the aged, to the sick and to the
happy," with small occasion for " danger, difficulty, and toil "—the delight of youth. Wherefore the flock, with only the son for black sheep,
must quit the fold, and see something of the
wicked world outside the garden. Their first
venture would seem harmless enough ; being no
farther than over the fields to Cleves Park, just
purchased by Uncle Sir Hugh, who had " inherited
from his ancestors an unencumbered estate of
£5,000 per annum."

" His temper was unalterably sweet, and every
thought of his breast was laid open to the world with
an almost infantine artlessness. But his talents bore
no proportion to the goodness of his heart, an insuper-
able want of quickness, and of application in his early
days, having left him, at a later period, wholly unculti-
vated, and singularly self-formed."

Mrs. Tyrold found occasion for further delight
in the " superiority " of her husband ; " though
she was not insensible to the fair future prospects
of her children, which seemed the probable result
of this change of abode." Both parents, indeed,
prove unexpectedly " worldly " on this point ;
and though obviously far above the sacrifice of

principle for *profit,* they permit their offspring
to run risks—as they deem them—in their com-
plaisance to a rich relative.

Sir Hugh is a very prodigy of indiscretion, and
complicates matters by the introduction of more
cousins — Indiana Lynmere, an empty-headed but
" most exquisite workmanship of nature,'' and
her wicked brother Clermont ; who were his wards.
A young orphan of great wealth, Edgar Mandlebert, pupil and ward of the Rev. Tyrold, completes
the group ; though mischief is made, and all com-
plications really inaugurated, by Indiana's silly
governess, Miss Margland.

Obviously there are two main issues at stake—
the property of Sir Hugh, and the hand of Edgar.
Miss Margland desires both for her favourite,
and evinces much ingenuity in the pursuit.   The
worthy baronet, however, does not long hesitate
about the estate.   He designs it originally for
Camilla, simply because she charms him most,
and, with his customary naïveté, lets all the world
into the secret.   Then, by his own absurd thought-
lessness, he suffers the " little sister Eugenia ''
to catch the smallpox ; and by ill-timed play-
fulness, lames her for life.   Heart-broken with

remorse, and perfectly confident in Camilla's generous disinterestedness, he promptly compensates the poor child by making *her* his heiress; and, after again announcing his intentions in public, proves unexpectedly resolute in maintaining them to the end. By outsiders, however, it is occasionally still supposed that all his money will go to Camilla; and, consequently, she has some experience of fortune-hunters.

The character of Eugenia deserves notice. She is quite unlike Camilla, and the differences are no doubt accentuated by the combination of disease and deformity which, shutting her out from the obvious distractions of "youth," afford much time for solitary reflection. Her uncle, moreover, provided her with a scholarly tutor, and to Lionel she was always "dear little Greek and Latin." It was, indeed, this highly educated, but very youthful, paragon on whom her own family depended at every crisis, whose advice they followed, whose opinion they sought, whose approval was their standard of conduct and feeling. Younger than Camilla, she was more mature, more thoughtful and clear-headed, always decided and always right. Curiously enough, these young people seldom

W.N.   D

consulted their parents, they went to Eugenia ;
and she, in the most important crisis of her life,
actually *opposed* the judgment of her elders, de-
manding from herself a sacrifice which even their
lofty ideal did not expect or commend. They
considered her mistaken, but "they knew she
must do what she thought right," and they sadly
acquiesced.

Yet there were no Spartan heroics about Eugenia.
She had even more "sensibility" than Camilla,
far more romance, and was more easily deceived.
Among other schemes of repentance for the injuries
he had so innocently inflicted on her, Sir Hugh
"arranged" for her to marry Clermont Lynmere,
before that young gentleman had come home ;
and, of course, informed the whole household
of his project. Such was Eugenia's extravagant
refinement in romance, that, though she could not
avoid being attracted by the most obviously in-
sincere raptures of young men in want of her
fortune, one of them "kissing her hand she
thought a *liberty most unpardonable.* She regarded
it as an injury to Clermont, that would risk his
life should he ever know it, *and a blot to her own
delicacy,* as irreparable as it was irremediable."

It is obvious that such excessive refinement proves ill-fitted to combat the unprincipled ambitions of the other sex, incited by her uncle's generosity; and when the villain, feigning a passion well calculated to stir her fancy, threatens to blow out his brains if she refuse him, we do not read of her yielding with surprise. To her notion a promise given under any circumstances is absolutely binding; and when, undeceived, she is recommended by her pious parents to repudiate it, the heroic martyr remains steadfast, and suffers much through some volumes. Yet even in that extremity she proves a rock to her more wavering elder sister.

We have wandered too long, however, from our heroine.

"Camilla was, in secret, the fondest hope of her mother, though the rigour of her justice scarce permitted the partiality to beat even in her own breast. Nor did the happy little person need the avowed distinction. The tide of youthful glee flowed jocund from her heart, and the transparency of her fine blue veins almost showed the velocity of its current. Every look was a smile, every step was a spring, every thought was a hope, every feeling was joy! and the early felicity of her mind was without alloy. . . . The beauty of Camilla, though neither perfect nor regular,

had an influence peculiar on the beholder, it was hard
to catch its fault ; and the cynic connoisseur, who
might persevere in seeking it, would involuntarily
surrender the strict rules of his art to the predominance of its loveliness. Even judgment itself, the
coolest and last betrayed of our faculties, she took
by surprise, though it was not till she was absent the
seizure was detected. Her disposition was ardent in
sincerity, her mind untainted with evil. The reigning
and radical defect of her character—an imagination
that submitted to no control—proved not any antidote
against her attractions : it caught, by its force and
fire, the quick-kindling admiration of the lively ; it
possessed, by magnetic persuasion, the witchery to
create sympathy in the most serious."

It is a picture of an ideal, stammeringly defined
by Edgar : " The utmost vivacity of sentiment,
all the charm of soul, eternally beaming in the
eyes, playing in every feature, glowing in the
complexion, and brightening every smile."

Obviously hero and heroine are born for each
other. He admires her above all women, himself
has every perfection. And though Mrs. Tyrold
may have " gloried in the virtuous delicacy of her
daughter, that so properly, *till it was called for*,
concealed her tenderness from the object who
so deservingly inspired it," the reader can feel no

doubt, from the beginning, of her decided "partiality."

There are two obstacles, however, between the
lovers. In the first place, Edgar's tutor had twice
been deceived by women ; and so acts upon his
loyal pupil, by the urgent recommendation of
caution and delay, that he becomes " a creature
whose whole composition is a pile of accumulated
punctilios " ; one who " will spend his life in
refining away his own happiness." It is obvious
that, left to herself, Camilla's nature would bear
the closest inspection, as even the old misanthrope
ultimately admits. But Miss Margland cannot
endure any rivalry with Indiana, the " beautiful
vacant-looking cousin " who has been taught to
consider herself irresistible, though it is not quite
clear what Miss Burney would have her readers
believe as to the power of beauty. At one point
she declares that " a very young man seldom likes
a silly wife. It is generally when he is further
advanced in life that he takes that depraved taste.
He then flatters himself a fool will be easier to
govern." But elsewhere we are told that

" Men are always enchanted with something that is
both pretty and silly · because they can so easily

please and so soon disconcert it ; and when they have made the little blooming fools blush and look down, they feel nobly superior, and pride themselves in victory. . . . A man looks enchanted while his beautiful young bride talks nonsense ; it comes so prettily from her ruby lips, and she blushes and dimples with such lovely attraction while she utters it ; he casts his eyes around him with conscious elation to see her admirers, and his enviers."

The wily governess has all the audacity of a born diplomatist. She simply informs Sir Hugh, who always believes everybody, that Edgar is " practically " engaged to her pet pupil. The old man regards the matter as settled, and, in perfect innocence, encourages her machinations to make a fact of her desire—the girl herself being flattered into an indifferent accomplice.

Now Camilla had acquired the habit, quite becoming to girlhood, of looking to Edgar, more or less consciously, for guidance through life, and of actually asking his advice on all delicate, or doubtful, occasions. Miss Margland ingeniously accuses her of trying to catch the heir by these " confidences," and Sir Hugh, without for one moment acknowledging the possibility of Camilla having a bad motive, advises her to avoid even the appearance of jealousy, and leave Indiana a fair field. Such an appeal to her generosity, from so kind a friend, was sure of eager support ; and the unfortunate girl is thus driven to seek friends against whom Edgar had warned her, and to assume the character of capriciousness and instability. This proves her Introduction to the Great World, whither Miss Burney hurries all her heroines. Like the rest, she arrives entirely unprepared, parents of those days apparently not considering either advice or guidance on such matters a part of their duty. Framed for innocent pleasure, her natural gaiety and ardent temperament lead her astray in every direction. She remains entirely unsoiled, but invariably does the wrong thing. She gets into debt, through sheer ignorance and humility ; she makes friends of " doubtful " people, through pity and innocence ; she even follows the advice of a worldly acquaintance, attempting to move her lover by flirting with other men. Every word and action is designed to please him : all have the contrary effect. His heart remains faithful ; his reason must criticise.

At this stage of the work Miss Burney revives somewhat of her first, spontaneous, manner. The descriptions of Society—wherein " *Ton*, in the scale of connoisseurs in *certain circles,* is as much above fashion, as fashion is above fortune "—are animated and amusing. We are introduced to many new types, male and female, naïvely exaggerated perhaps in detail, but absolutely alive and cunningly varied. The " prevailing ill-manners of the leaders in the *ton* " astonish, no less than their brutal cowardice—in face of a *girl's* danger—disgusts. Fine gentlemen, it would seem, are neither gallant nor chivalrous. The ladies, indeed, are not much better. A divinity, unequally yoked, " excites every hope by a *sposo* [1] properly detestable —yet gives birth to despair by a coldness the most shivering." Less favoured beauties are equally vain, and some of them more indiscreet.

But here, as in *Cecilia,* our author cannot resist the indulgence of heroics. She is not satisfied with her delightful " Comedy of Manners," with the ordinary misunderstandings and heart-burnings essential to romance. In her later volumes she plunges Camilla, and the whole Tyrold family, into the wildest distress. They lose all their money ; Eugenia's husband commits suicide ;

[1] The " *caro sposo* " of Mrs. Elton.

Lionel nearly murders an uncle, from whom he had expectations, by a practical joke ; and Camilla acquires, by an over-elaborated series of foolish impulses, the appearance of having injured her parents beyond forgiveness. Immersed in difficulties, and not in the least understanding the circumstances, her father and mother refuse to see her ; and the forsaken maiden prays for death. The whole episode is given in Miss Burney's worst manner, tempting the reader to mere angry impatience with so much false sentiment and senseless emotion.   They tremble, they faint, they weep, they see visions ; we could almost fancy ourselves in Bedlam.

In the end, of course, Edgar comes back, receives an " explanation " from Camilla—written, as she supposed, on her death-bed ; and promptly restores everybody to their senses and, incidentally— having plenty to spare—to prosperity.

" Thus ended the long conflicts, doubts, suspenses, and sufferings of Edgar and Camilla; who, without one inevitable calamity, one unavoidable distress, so nearly fell the sacrifice to the two extremes of Imprudence, and Suspicion, to the natural heedlessness of youth unguided, or to the acquired distrust of experience that had been wounded."

At first sight, certainly, it would seem that we had little here of the Richardson-realism, and that Miss Burney was challenging comparison, in their own field, with such melodramatic romancists as Mrs. Radcliffe. Yet Camilla, and even Eugenia, are far more like real life than Emily St. Aubert. However extravagantly composed, they are *founded on* nature, whereas the older novelists worked entirely from imagination. Before Richardson (and here, of course, Mrs. Radcliffe belongs to the earlier age) the models for character were not drawn from experience and observation. There was, it would seem, a preconceived notion, and certain accepted rules, for the " make-up " of heroes, heroines, parents, villains and the rest— which are somewhat akin to the constructed ideal of abstract Beauty favoured by certain art critics. They were prepared, without very much reference to actual humanity, from mysteriously acquired recipes of virtue and vice.

We cannot find any reason to believe that Miss Burney ever worked, in her most " exalted " moments, on such a plan. She idealised from life, not from the imagination. She really believed that the young ladies of her acquaintance all aimed, more or less consciously, at that exquisite delicacy which she delighted to exhibit; and, in all probability, she was justified in her faith. Her rhapsodies are sincere; and they obviously apply to her own sentiments, shared by her contemporaries. They are—in their own very feminine fashion—reflections on reality—not creations of art by any accepted canons.

And the very exaggerated artificiality of *Camilla* makes it more typical—of herself and her period—than *Evelina* or *Cecilia*: and therefore more representative of Woman, when she began to write fiction for herself. The genius of her earlier work carried it some way in advance of its time; although the progress of her immediate successors is most remarkable. Camilla is the very essence of eighteenth-century girlhood; ill-mated, as they were no doubt, to "our present race of young men," whose "frivolous fickleness nauseates whatever they can reach"; who—when they are not heroes—"have a weak shame of asserting, or even listening to what is right, and a shallow pride in professing and performing what is wrong."

It is instructive, indeed, to observe with what apparent crudity Miss Burney has chosen to illustrate the greater purity and refinement, the superior moral standard, of women to those of men : a problem which seems to have almost vanished with Jane Austen (though we may detect it at work under the surface), and which has reappeared so prominently, after quite a new fashion, 'in modern literature. By the men novelists this was practically assumed without comment ; but our knowledge of facts would seem to warrant the emphasis awarded the question by women in their opening campaign of the pen. Here, as elsewhere, Miss Burney was almost the first to teach us what women actually thought and felt : in marked contrast to what it had been hitherto considered becoming for them to express. She was, always, and everywhere, the mouthpiece of her sex.

And, finally, because she was not an " instructed " or professional writer, and had not studied good literature, we must recognise the real, great, drawback of *Camilla* : its grandiloquent style. Dr. Johnson did much for English prose : his ultimate influence was towards vigour, simplicity, clearness, and common sense. But he was personally pompous, a whale in the dictionary ; and those who copied him without discretion only made themselves ridiculous. It would be easy enough to find parallels in *Rasselas*, and elsewhere, for all the clumsy inversions and stilted antitheses of *Camilla*. But here we can only regret the blindness of ignorant hero-worship, and the natural, if foolish, desire to please or flatter by imitation. Miss Burney wrote Johnsonese fluently, and thereby ruined her natural powers. We cannot estimate, by her foolishness, the influence of the Dictator.

Imitation has not been, fortunately, the besetting sin of women novelists, and we may pass over this one " terrible example " without further comment.

"CECILIA" TO "SENSE AND SENSIBILITY"

(1782–1811)

IN considering the women writers immediately following Miss Burney, we are confronted at the outset with a deliberate return to the methods of composition in vogue before Richardson If MRS. RADCLIFFE (1764–1823) employs, as she does, Defoe-like minuteness of detail in description, she entitles all her works " Romances," and is fully justified in that nomenclature. " It was the cry at the period," says her biographer, " and has sometimes been repeated since, that the romances of Mrs. Radcliffe, and the applause with which they were received, were evil signs of the times, and argued a great and increasing degradation of the public taste, which, instead of banqueting as heretofore upon scenes of passion, like those of Richardson, or of life and manners, as in the pages of Smollett and Fielding, was now coming back to the fare of the nursery, and gorged upon the wild and improbable fictions of an over-heated imagination."

Yet the anonymous author of the *Pursuits of Literature* writes of some sister-novelists : " Though all of them are ingenious ladies, yet they are too frequently whining and frisking in novels, till our girls' heads turn wild with impossible adventures. Not so the mighty magician of *The Mysteries of Udolpho*, bred and nourished by the Florentine muses in their sacred solitary caverns, amid the paler shrines of Gothic superstition, and in all the dreariness of enchantment : a poetess whom Ariosto would with rapture have acknowledged, as

'. . . La nudrita
Damigella Trivulzia al sacro speco.' "—O.F. c. xlvi.

We fear to-day it would be difficult to find men " too mercurial to be delighted " by Richardson, " too dull to comprehend " Le Sage, " too saturnine to relish " Fielding, who would yet " with difficulty be divorced from *The Romance of the Forest* " : since every one of us now

" boasts an English heart,
Unused at ghosts or rattling bones to start."

Jane Austen, of course, could never have written

Northanger Abbey had she not enjoyed Mrs.
Radcliffe ; and we say at once that those delightfully absurd chapters in which Catherine is allowed
to indulge in the most unfounded suspicions of
General Tilney, are not substantially unfair to
the famous wife of William Radcliffe, Esq. ; as the
artless conversations between Miss Morland and
Miss Thorpe no doubt justly reflect the deep
interest excited by her stories in the young and
inexperienced. We do not readily, to-day, admire
so much " exuberance and fertility of imagination " :
we have little, or no, patience with " adventures
heaped on adventures in quick and brilliant suc-
cession, with all the hairbreadth charms of escape
or capture," resembling some " splendid Oriental
tale."

But there can be no question that Mrs. Radcliffe
achieved, in three admirable examples, a perfectly
legitimate attempt—the establishment of that
School of Terror inaugurated by no less brilliant
a writer than Horace Walpole (in his *Castle of
Otranto*, 1764), and seldom revived in England
with any success.

It is true that very careful criticism of her
methods may discover their artificiality. " Her

heroines voluntarily expose themselves to situations which, in nature, a lonely female would certainly have avoided. They are too apt to choose the midnight hour for investigating the mysteries of a deserted chamber or secret passage, and generally are only supplied," like Mr. Pickwick, " with an expiring lamp when about to read the most interesting documents." But Emily St. Aubert is not surely designed for comparison with even that " imbecility in females " which Henry Tilney declared to be " a great enhancement of their personal charms." She is a heroine, not a woman ; and if, unlike Walpole, Mrs. Radcliffe demands, and supplies, a material explanation of all supernatural appearances, she yet allows her imagination to wander freely over the realms of superstitious alarm, wherein the *reason* of woman cannot presumably hold sway. Certainly, had Emily been less impulsive she would have missed many opportunities of proving herself courageous.

I cannot myself, however, entirely avoid the impression that, in their natural desire for classification, the critics have laid undue stress on Mrs. Radcliffe's use of Mystery. In the three hundred and four, double column, pages of *Udolpho* there are, besides occasional voices, only three definite examples of this artifice—the waxen figure behind the veil, the moving pall, and the disappearance of Ludovico. The main plot is really no more than a spirited example of the conventional Romance-plan (in the development of which she is wittily said to have invented Lord Byron)—an involved narrative of terrible sufferings and dangers incurred by an immaculate heroine, of unmeasured tyranny and violence exerted by a melancholy villain, of protracted misunderstandings concerning the gallant hero, with hurried explanations all round in the last chapter to justify the wedding-bells.

Obviously there is no realism here. Everything depends upon conscious exaggeration : whether it be a description of " the Apennines in their darkest horrors," or of a " gloomy and sublime " castle's " mouldering walls " ; of crime indulged without restraint, or innocence unsullied by the world. Montoni is not more inhuman in his passion than Emily in the " tender elevation of her mind."

For despite the most solemn warnings of St. Aubert (quoted above), his Emily has far more sensibility than any of Miss Burney's heroines, and exemplifies the dangerous doctrine that " virtue and taste are nearly the same." She and Valancourt, indeed, were indifferent to " the frivolities of common life " ; their " ideas were simple and grand, like the landscapes among which they moved " ; their sentiments spontaneously " arranged themselves " in original verse.

The fact is, that Scott's startlingly generous estimate suggests several sound conclusions : by dwelling upon the genuine poetical feeling to be observed in Mrs. Radcliffe's romances, and the sincerity of her sympathy with nature. Though it has been remarked, with some justice, that " as her story is usually enveloped in mystery, so there is, as it were, a haze over her landscapes " ; and that, " were six artists to attempt to embody the Castle of Udolpho upon canvas, they would probably produce six drawings entirely dissimilar to each other, all of them equally authorised by the printed description."

MRS. INCHBALD (1753–1821), on the other hand, followed the new school in writing simple narratives of everyday life ; but she produced little more than a pale imitation of *The Man of Feeling*

(1771), by Henry Mackenzie, the only masculine
exponent of "sensibility"; though her *Simple
Story* (1791) and *Nature and Art* (1796) have been
frequently reprinted. She aimed at dissecting
the human heart, as Richardson had done ; and
there is, admittedly, a certain melodramatic, and
almost decadent, charm in her work.

MARIA EDGEWORTH (1767–1849) was, certainly,
the most prominent of our novelists between Fanny
Burney and Jane Austen. Being a girl of eleven
when *Evelina* was published, she lived to witness
the triumph of *Vanity Fair*. Living beyond her
eighth decade, she produced over sixty books.
Having inspired Scott, on his own testimony, to
the production of the Waverley Novels, she actually
inaugurated, promoted, or established at least
four forms of fiction more or less new to her
contemporaries.

Like Fanny Burney, she owed much to the
enthusiasm and example of a liberal-minded and
cultured father : that Richard Lovell Edgeworth
who married several of the young persons whom
the author of *Sandford and Merton* had educated
for the honour of his own hand. He and Day
were notable scholastic reformers, and the in-

fluence of their innumerable theories on life and the Pedagogue, largely imported from over the Channel, is everywhere visible in Maria's work.

Richard Lovell actually collaborated in the two volumes, inspired by Rousseau's *Émile*, on *Practical Education* (1798), and supplied forewords of edification to that marvellous series in which she first proved the possibility of training the young idea by ethical storiettes which were *not* tracts. That most clumsily named *Parents' Assistant* (1801), the *Moral Tales* of the same year, and the fascinating *Frank*, are still nursery classics deserving of immortality. We may not, to-day, accept without protest many of the " lessons " which they were designed to enforce ; but their sympathetic insight into the nature of the child (with which recently we have been so much concerned), the attractive simplicity and dramatic interest of the direct narrative, set an example, from the very foundations of juvenile literature, which has borne plentiful fruit.

It should be noticed, moreover, in this connection that Miss Edgeworth had already produced a spirited defence of female education (*Letters to Literary Ladies*, 1795) ; while she soon followed in the footsteps of Fanny Burney by writing most lively satires on *fin de siècle* Society, pointed with travesties of French "naturalism," of which the chief, perhaps, is *Belinda*, published in 1801; and further extended the scope of the modern novel by the introduction of the finished Short Story, under the attractive heading of *Tales of Fashionable Life*.

And, finally, besides again collaborating with her father in an *Essay on Irish Bulls* (1802), she produced that stimulating " Irish Brigade," which banished the " stage " Patrick from literature, introduced genuine Celtic types, such as Coney, King of the Black Isles; and, by creating the " national " novel, may be regarded as the legitimate parent of what their illustrious author so modestly offered to the public as " something of the same kind for his own country."

Although just failing everywhere to reveal genius, Miss Edgeworth reflects, with marvellous versatility, all the intellectual movements of her generation. Adopting, and adapting to her own purposes, the " form for women " set out by Miss Burney, she widened its application to the discussion of social and political problems, and was the first to make fiction a picture not only of life, but of its meaning. In fact she forestalled no less for adults, than for the young, that vast array of consciously didactic narrative which threatens, in our own time, to bury beyond revival the original, and the supreme, inspiration of Art in Literature—to give pleasure.

The humour, the pathos, the knowledge of the world, and, above all, the common sense regulating Miss Edgeworth's work, have not secured her as permanent a popularity as she justly merits. But, if we do not, to-day, frequently read even *Ormond*, *The Absentee*, or *Castle Rackrent*, the occasions which gratefully recall their accomplished author to our remembrance are most astonishingly frequent.

Of HANNAH MORE (1745–1833) most readers probably know even far less than of Maria Edgeworth ; and her work can only claim notice in this place on account of the energy with which she followed Miss Edgeworth's lead in didactic fiction. Accustomed to the society of fashionable blue-stockings (then a comparative novelty in London life), she exposed their foibles with considerable humour in private correspondence ; while her plays were cheerfully staged by Garrick. But awakened, in later life, to the sin of play-going, she became known for her vigorous tracts (inspiring, by turns, the foundation of Sunday schools and of the Religious Tract Society), until she published, at sixty-four, her one novel entitled *Cœlebs in Search of a Wife.*

If this somewhat ponderous effusion does not altogether deserve the satirical onslaught with which Sydney Smith heralded in the *Edinburgh* its first appearance, we cannot claim for the author any particular skill in construction or much fidelity to real life.   It is, in fact, no more than a " dramatic sermon," and a sermon, moreover, in support of narrow-minded sectarianism.   As the reviewer informs us, " Cœlebs wants a wife . . . who may add materially to the happiness of his future life. His first journey is to London, where, in the midst of the gay society of the metropolis, of course, he does not find a wife ; and his next journey is to the family of Mr. Stanley, the head of the Methodists, a serious people, where, of course, he does find a wife."   That is the whole story.   We must submit, in the meantime, to diatribes, pronounced by the virtuous, against dancing, theatres, cards, assemblies, and frivolous conversation, until we are in danger of losing all interest in the persons of the tale.

It is enough for us, in fact, to mark a niche for Miss More in the development of women's work; only remembering the great service she rendered her generation by a rarely sympathetic understanding of the poor as individual human beings.

A STUDY IN FINE ART

(JANE AUSTEN, 1775–1817)

WITH Jane Austen we reach the centre of our subject : the establishment of the Woman's School, the final expression of domesticity. If not, perhaps, more essentially feminine than Fanny Burney, she is more womanly. The charming girlishness of *Evelina* has here matured into a grown-up sisterly attitude towards humanity, which, without being either quite worldly or at all pedantic, is yet artistically composed. Whether consciously or not, she has spoken—within her chosen province—the last word for all women for all time. There is no comment on life, no picture of manners, no detail of characterisation—either humorous or sympathetic—which a man could have expressed in these precise words. Woman is openly the centre of her world ; and, if men are more to her than fireside pets, she is only concerned with them as an element (or rather the chief element) in the life of women.

66

The comparison, already instituted, between the man-made " feminines " of *Pamela* and *Clarissa Harlowe* with Miss Burney's " young ladies," may be applied to Elizabeth Bennet and Emma Woodhouse with added emphasis in every particular. The " woman " in them is more modern, nearer the heart of humanity, but still spontaneously of that sex.

" To say the truth," confesses a contemporary reviewer, " we suspect one of Miss Austen's great merits in our eyes to be the insight she gives us into the peculiarities of female character. Authoresses can scarcely ever forget the *esprit de corps*—can scarcely ever forget that they *are authoresses*. They seem to feel a sympathetic shudder at exposing naked a female mind. *Elles se peignent en buste*, and leave the mysteries of womanhood to be described by some interloping male, like Richardson or Marivaux, who is turned out before he has seen half the rites, and is forced to spin from his own conjectures the rest. Now from this fault Miss Austen is free. Her heroines are what one knows women must be, though one never can get them to acknowledge it. As liable ' to fall in love first,' as anxious to attract the attention of an agreeable man, as much taken with a striking manner, or a handsome face, as unequally gifted with constancy and firmness, as liable to have their affections biased by convenience or fashion, as we, on our part, will admit men to be. As some illustration of what we mean, we refer our

readers to the conversation between Miss Crawford
and Fanny (vol. iii. p. 102); Fanny's meeting with
her father (p. 199); her reflection after reading
Edmund's letter (p. 246); her happiness (good, and
heroine though she be), in the midst of the miseries of
all her friends, when she finds that Edmund has decidedly broken with her rival; feelings, all of them,
which, under the influence of strong passion, must
alloy the purest mind, but with which scarcely any
authoress but Miss Austen would have ventured to
temper the œtherial materials of a heroine."

Again, Miss Burney, as we have seen, had first
made it possible for a woman to write novels and
be respectable. Yet even with her, authorship was
something of an adventure. Her earliest manuscripts were solemnly burnt, as in repentance for
frivolity, before her sorrowing sisters; needlework
was ordained every morning by a not tyrannical
stepmother; social duties occupied most afternoons
and evenings. And if she *must* write, Dr. Burney
was always ready enough at dictation, and any
lady might act as secretary to such a father without
reproach.

In the outside world, when her success was won,
we can detect a similar attitude. The authoress
of *Evelina*, indeed, was taken up everywhere and
universally petted; but even literary Society never

regarded her quite as one of themselves. We feel that she was always on show among them—a kind of freak, like the girl who cried to order at dinner-parties without spoiling her complexion ; welcomed, but not admitted—as were actors, musicians, and others born and bred for the amusement of the great.

She herself never resumed work for its own sake after the first flush of popularity, in which she composed *Cecilia*. As lady-in-waiting, bored by tiresome punctilio ; as Madame D'Arblay, happy in simple domesticity ; her pen lay idle save when exercised by filial piety or specifically to earn money. The later novels were pure hack-work, obviously lacking in spontaneity.

It was reserved for Jane Austen, the daughter of a later generation, though actually dying before Miss Burney, to establish finally the position of woman as a professional novelist. True, she was even more domestic than her predecessor, and entirely without what we should regard as the necessary training or experience. Her family were seldom aware of the time given to work, simply because it never occurred to her that she might claim privacy or resent interruption. But they

took a keen interest in the results, and evidence
exists in abundance of their reading every completed volume with enthusiasm.

Of her own attitude towards her work, and of
its reception with the public, there can be no
doubt. She always regarded herself, and was regarded, as a professional. Circumstances might
induce temporary silence, because she was domestic,
modest, and affectionate ; but if Jane Austen never
complained—and we hear of no protest at the extraordinary delay in their appearance—we may be
quite sure the novels were written for the public, by
whom she felt confident one day of being read.
The style is obviously spontaneous, of which the
writing itself meant keen enjoyment ; but the
work was not done merely for the pleasure of
doing it. It was her life—not because of any
disappointment in love, if she experienced such,
but because genius such as hers demands self-
expression and commands a hearing. From*the
beginning, moreover, no one stopped to marvel
that a woman could do so well : they judged her as
an artist among her peers.

Jane Austen had none of the advantages of Miss
Burney, who knew everybody, including the wig-

maker next door. Apparently she took little interest in politics or social problems; and our ideals of culture suffer shock before her allusions to *The Spectator*, to read and admire which she holds the affectation of a blue-stocking. Admittedly she was a voracious novel-reader, but for her own pleasure merely; certainly not with any idea of historical development or artistic criticism. In all probability even her study of human nature was spontaneous and unconscious.

Yet she expected to be taken seriously. Miss Burney had ventured an apology for her art—a plea as woman to men which was daring enough for her generation, but still an apology. Miss Austen, speaking as much for the authoress of *Evelina* as for herself, shows far more confidence. She enlarges upon the skill and the labour involved in writing a novel, for which *honour is due*.[1] What she demands has been given her in full measure to overflowing. How closely her stories have wound themselves about the hearts of every successive generation, it were idle to measure or estimate. They are a part of our inheritance: appreciation is reckoned a test of culture.

[1] Both passages are quoted on page 129.

In the perfection, or development, of the methods inaugurated by Samuel Richardson—particularly as applied by women-writers—she also stands supreme. She entirely avoids criminals, melodrama, or any form of excitement. She does not even demand sensibility from her common-sense heroines.

While a woman was thus placing the cornerstone to the rise of domestic realism, man accomplished a glorious revival of Romanticism. Scott was born only four years before Jane Austen: *Waverley* and *Mansfield Park* were published in the same year. Fortunately we are able to form an accurate estimate of the impression her work produced upon her great contemporary, since the earliest serious appreciation of Jane was actually written by Sir Walter, and opens with a most instructive comparison between the "former rules of the novel" and "a class of fictions which has arisen," as he expresses it, "almost in our times." The article appeared in the *Quarterly Review*, October 1815; and it is very significant for us to notice that Scott places *Peregrine Pickle* and *Tom Jones* in the "old school," dating the new style only "fifteen or twenty years" back.

" In its first appearance, the novel was the legitimate
child of the romance ; and though the manners and
general turn of the composition were altered so as to
suit modern times, the author remained fettered by many
peculiarities derived from the original style of romantic
fiction. These may be chiefly traced in the conduct of
the narrative, and the tone of sentiment attributed to
the fictitious personages.   On the first point, although

> ' The talisman and magic wand were broke,
> Knights, dwarfs, and genii vanish'd into smoke,'

still the reader expected to peruse a course of adventures of a nature more interesting and extraordinary
than those which occur in his own life, or that of his
next-door neighbour.   The hero no longer defeated
armies by his single sword, clove giants to the chine,
or gained kingdoms. But he was expected to go through
perils by sea and land, to be steeped in poverty, to
be tried by temptation, to be exposed to the alternate
vicissitudes of adversity and prosperity, and his life
was a troubled scene of suffering and achievement.
Few novelists, indeed, adventured to deny to the hero
his final hour of tranquillity and happiness, though it
was the prevailing fashion never to relieve him out of
his last and most dreadful distress until the finishing
chapters of his history ; so that although his prosperity
in the record of his life was short, we were bound to
believe it was long and uninterrupted when the author
had done with him. The heroine was usually condemned to equal hardships and hazards. She was
regularly exposed to being forcibly carried off like a
Sabine virgin by some frantic admirer. And even if

she escaped the terrors of masked ruffians, an insidious
ravisher, a cloak wrapped forcibly around her head, and
a coach with the blinds [down] driving she could not
conjecture whither, she had still her share of wandering,
of poverty, of obloquy, of seclusion, and of imprisonment, and was frequently extended upon a bed of
sickness, and reduced to her last shilling before the
author condescended to shield her from persecution.
In all these dread contingencies the mind of the reader
was expected to sympathise, since by incidents so
much beyond the bounds of his ordinary experience,
his wonder and interest ought at once to be excited.
But gradually he became familiar with the land of
fiction, the adventures of which he assimilated not
with those of real life, but with each other. Let the
distress of the hero or heroine be ever so great,
the reader reposed an imperturbable confidence in the
talents of the author, who, as he had plunged them
into distress, would in his own good time, and when
things, as Tony Lumkin says, were in a concatenation
accordingly, bring his favourites out of all their troubles.
Mr. Crabbe has expressed his own and our feelings
excellently on this subject.

> ' For should we grant these beauties all endure
> Severest pangs, they've still the speediest cure ;
> Before one charm be wither'd from the face,
> Except the bloom which shall again have place,
> In wedlock ends each wish, in triumph all disgrace.
> And life to come, we fairly may suppose,
> One light bright contrast to these wild dark woes.'

" In short, the author of novels was, in former times,
expected to tread pretty much in the limits between

the concentric circles of probability and possibility ;
and as he was not permitted to transgress the latter,
his narrative, to make amends, almost always went
beyond the bounds of the former. Now, although
it may be urged that the vicissitudes of human life
have occasionally led an individual through as many
scenes of singular fortune as are represented in the
most extravagant of these fictions, still the causes and
personages acting on these changes have varied with
the progress of the adventurer's fortune, and do not
present that combined plot, (the object of every skilful
novelist), in which all the more interesting individuals
of the dramatis personæ have their appropriate share
in the action and in bringing about the catastrophe.
Here, even more than in its various and violent changes
of fortune, rests the improbability of the novel.   The
life of man rolls forth like a stream from the fountain,
or it spreads out into tranquillity like a placid or
stagnant lake.   In the latter case, the individual grows
old among the characters with whom he was born,
and is contemporary,—shares precisely the sort of weal
and woe to which his birth destined him,—moves in
the same circle,—and, allowing for the change of seasons,
is influenced by, and influences the same class of persons
by which he was originally surrounded.   The man of
mark and of adventure, on the contrary, resembles,
in the course of his life, the river whose mid-current
and discharge into the ocean are widely removed from
each other, as well as from the rocks and wild flowers
which its fountains first reflected ; violent changes of
time, of place, and of circumstances, hurry him forward

from one scene to another, and his adventures will usually be found only connected with each other because they have happened to the same individual. Such a history resembles an ingenious, fictitious narrative, exactly in the degree in which an old dramatic chronicle of the life and death of some distinguished character, where all the various agents appear and disappear as in the page of history, approaches a regular drama, in which every person introduced plays an appropriate part, and every point of the action tends to one common catastrophe.

"We return to the second broad line of distinction between the novel, as formerly composed, and real life, —the difference, namely, of the sentiments. The novelist professed to give an imitation of nature, but it was, as the French say, *la belle nature*. Human beings, indeed, were presented, but in the most senti- mental mood, and with minds purified by a sensibility which often verged on extravagance. In the serious class of novels, the hero was usually

'A knight or lover, who never broke a vow.'

And although, in those of a more humorous cast, he was permitted a licence, borrowed either from real life or from the libertinism of the drama, still a distinc- tion was demanded even from Peregrine Pickle, or Tom Jones ; and the hero, in every folly of which he might be guilty, was studiously vindicated from the charge of infidelity of the heart. The heroine was, of course, still more immaculate ; and to have conferred her affections upon any other than the lover to whom the reader had destined her from their first meeting,

would have been a crime against sentiment which no
author, of moderate prudence, would have hazarded,
under the old *régime*.

" Here, therefore, we have two essential and important circumstances, in which the earlier novels
differed from those now in fashion, and were more
nearly assimilated to the old romances. And there
can be no doubt that, by the studied involution and
extrication of the story, by the combination of incidents
new, striking and wonderful beyond the course of
ordinary life, the former authors opened that obvious
and strong sense of interest which arises from curiosity ;
as by the pure, elevated, and romantic cast of the
sentiment, they conciliated those better propensities
of our nature which loves to contemplate the picture
of virtue, even when confessedly unable to imitate
its excellences.

" But strong and powerful as these sources of emotion
and interest may be, they are, like all others, capable
of being exhausted by habit. The imitators who
rushed in crowds upon each path in which the great
masters of the art had successively led the way, produced upon the public mind the usual effect of satiety.
The first writer of a new class is, as it were, placed on
a pinnacle of excellence, to which, at the earliest glance
of a surprised admirer, his ascent seems little less than
miraculous.   Time and imitation speedily diminish the
wonder, and each successive attempt establishes a
kind of progressive scale of ascent between the lately
deified author, and the reader, who had deemed his
excellence inaccessible.   The stupidity, the mediocrity,

the merit of his imitators, are alike fatal to the first inventor, by showing how possible it is to exaggerate his faults and to come within a certain point of his beauties.

" Materials also (and the man of genius as well as his wretched imitator must work with the same) become stale and familiar. Social life, in our civilized days, affords few instances capable of being painted in the strong dark colours which excite surprise and horror ; and robbers, smugglers, bailiffs, caverns, dungeons, and mad-houses, have been all introduced until they cease to interest. And thus in the novel, as in every style of composition which appeals to the public taste, the more rich and easily worked mines being exhausted, the adventurous author must, if he is desirous of success, have recourse to those which were disdained by his predecessors as unproductive, or avoided as only capable of being turned to profit by great skill and labour.

" Accordingly a style of novel has arisen, within the last fifteen or twenty years, differing from the former in the points upon which the interest hinges ; neither alarming our credulity nor amusing our im- agination by wild variety of incident, or by those pictures of romantic affection and sensibility, which were formerly as certain attributes of fictitious char- acters as they are of rare occurrence among those who actually live and die. The substitute for these excitements, which had lost much of their poignancy by the repeated and injudicious use of them, was the art of copying from nature as she really exists in the common walks of life, and presenting to the reader, instead of the splendid scenes of an imaginary world, a correct and striking representation of that which is daily taking place around him.

" In adventuring upon this task, the author makes obvious sacrifices, and encounters peculiar difficulty. He who paints from *le beau idéal*, if his scenes and sentiments are striking and interesting, is in a great measure exempted from the difficult task of reconciling them with the ordinary probabilities of life : but he who paints a scene of common occurrence, places his composition within that extensive range of criticism which general experience offers to every reader. The resemblance of a statue of Hercules we must take on the artist's judgment ; but every one can criticize that which is presented as the portrait of a friend, or neighbour. Something more than a mere sign-post likeness is also demanded. The portrait must have spirit and character, as well as resemblance ; and being deprived of all that, according to Bayes, goes ' to elevate and surprize,' it must make amends by displaying depth of knowledge and dexterity of execution. We, therefore, bestow no mean compliment upon the author of *Emma*, when we say that, keeping close to common incidents, and to such characters as occupy the ordinary walks of life, she has produced sketches of such spirit and originality, that we never miss the excitation which depends upon a narrative of uncommon events, arising from the consideration of minds, manners and sentiments, greatly above our own. In this class she stands almost alone ; for the scenes of Miss Edgeworth are laid in higher life, varied

by more romantic incident, and by her remarkable
power of embodying and illustrating national character.
But the author of *Emma* confines herself chiefly to the
middling classes of society ; her most distinguished
characters do not rise greatly above well-bred country
gentlemen and ladies ; and those which are sketched
with most originality and precision, belong to a class
rather below that standard.   The narrative of all her
novels is composed of such common occurrences as may
have fallen under the observation of most folks ; and
her dramatis personæ conduct themselves upon the
motives and principles which the readers may re-
cognize as ruling their own and that of most of
their acquaintances."

It is manifestly clear to us, then, from these
passages, that Jane Austen's contemporaries were
quite aware of her influence upon the progress of
fiction ; and so generous a tribute, from one whose
mighty genius had set the current in other directions, must be accounted no less honourable to the
critic than to the criticised.

Four years after her death (*i.e.* six years later)
the new school is again applauded, in an admirable
appreciation, by Archbishop Whately of the
posthumous *Persuasion* and *Northanger Abbey*,[1]
who dwells at great length upon an important

[1] Also in the *Quarterly*, 1821.

distinction between the "unnatural" and the "merely improbable" in fiction.

Scott, of course, was always generous in criticism; and his striking enthusiasm for Mrs. Radcliffe and the earlier women-writers, in his *Lives of the Novelists*, reveals no less chivalrous gallantry than his famous tribute to Miss Edgeworth. Still it was obviously necessary for the great critic to *explain* the grounds of his enthusiasm; and the " more assured attitude of applause which Whateley was able to adopt, after so short an interval, may serve to witness the advance which her genius had achieved in the general estimate."

We cannot avoid noticing, however, that neither of her contemporary masculine critics seems to have been quite happy about the ideal of womanhood which Jane Austen was certainly the first to introduce. It required courage, indeed, to conceive of a heroine without "sensibility," and the creator of Marianne Dashwood must certainly have been perfectly conscious of the omission. It happens that Scott and Whateley were both thirty-four when these articles were written, yet each complains, after his own fashion, of the calculating prudence here revealed towards love and matrimony by the young ladies of the piece. One would have supposed that neither of them was either old enough to remember "sensibility" in real life, or young enough for idle dreaming. Clearly, however, they *had* a tender partiality for the old type, probably shared by their readers; although both writers assure us that young people in their day were not in fact at all addicted to the sacrifice of all for love.

Scott is certainly not justified in stating that Elizabeth was led to accept Darcy by discovering the grandeur of his estates, both because such an attitude was inconsistent with her mental independence, and because she herself jokingly suggests this explanation of the remarkable change in her sentiments towards him, to tease her sister.

But, on the other hand, Jane Austen's heroines may fairly be called cool and calculating in comparison with the poetical maidens of romance; and we have intentionally laboured this point at some length in order to emphasise the thoroughness with which reformers in fiction discarded the many artistic ornaments formerly used by story-tellers to enhance the "pleasures of imagination."

Every convention of romance was ruthlessly abandoned.

Later developments, as we shall see, introduced other elements which partially supplied these omissions, and once more removed the novel from pure realism; but it would almost seem as if Jane Austen had deliberately set herself to prove how much it was possible to do without. She admits neither unusual mixture of society, cultured allusion, nor morbid or criminal impulses. Like her immediate predecessors, she wilfully limits the variety of character-types by strictly confining herself to her own narrow experience—her groups of character are curiously similar, her plots repeat each other : she discards every source of excitement from adventure, mystery, or melodramatic emotion ; and, finally, she denies the hero or heroine any charm which may be derived from " sensibility " or romantic idealism. Hers is realism,[1] naked and unashamed ; challenging

[1] It is scarcely necessary, perhaps, to remark that the word " realism " is used, here and elsewhere, without any reference to the limited significance it has recently acquired. Realism, of course, really means truthfulness to life, *including* imagination, faith, poetry, and the ideal ; and *not* a photographic reproduction of certain unpleasant, more or less abnormal, phases of human nature.

comparison with life itself at every point, wholly dependent upon truthfulness to nature. Her triumph is purely artistic : the absolute fitness of expression to reveal insight, observation, sympathy, and humour ; in a simple narrative of parochial affairs, composed with rare skill, faithfully reflecting everyday life and ordinary people.

From such commonplace material she has woven a spell over the imagination and secured our warm interest in characters and episodes : much as the simplicity of English landscapes will hold our affection against the claims of nature's grandest magnificence.

Detailed analysis of her six " studies from life " will serve only to increase our wonder, and may be indulged without fear of reversed, or even qualified, judgment.

Inevitably Jane Austen scribbled in girlhood—too busily, according to her own judgment ; but the printed fragments are *not* specially precocious, and we have no right to judge so careful an artist by work she left unfinished or rejected with deliberation, however interesting in itself.

As we all know, without having any clue to

the explanation, she found herself rather suddenly, while still a young woman ; and did all her work in two surprisingly brief periods—sharply separated, and each responsible for three novels, two full length and one much shorter. *Pride and Prejudice*, her first finished production, has every appearance of maturity, and reveals the principal qualities which characterised her to the end.

This novel, by many considered her greatest work, is primarily—like *Evelina* and *Cecilia*—a study in manners. Its aim is frankly to amuse : the dominant note is irresponsible gaiety : the appeal is more intellectual than emotional. Certainly we are interested in the story, we have considerable affection for the characters : but it does not excite passion, stimulate philosophic reflection, or stir imagination. We find here no solutions to any vexed social problem. Past mistress she is in the great art of story-telling, and a supreme stylist ; yet the authoress seems always content to skim the surface of things, taking no thought of storm or fire below.

Miss Austen is no cynic : she certainly detests coarseness : yet Lydia's fall and its consequences,

round which any modern novelist would have
centred the whole picture, is handled with something very like levity. We can scarcely avoid
amazement at the astonishingly vulgar attitude
of Mrs. Bennet or at Mary's appalling priggishness
on the occasion : but such serious thoughts do not
retain us long.   In reality we are chiefly interested
in the possible effects of the girl's folly upon her
elder sisters—will it, or will it not, separate
them for ever from the men they love ? It is
only a few quiet words of unselfish sympathy
from Jane, easily forgotten by most of us, that
reveal the sentiments of the authoress on such
questions—with which, apparently, she holds
that fiction has little concern.

Primarily, however, we are attracted by *Pride
and Prejudice* as a work of art. The unfailing
humour and pointed wit, the marvellous aptness
of every polished phrase, hold us spellbound.
The very first sentence plunges us right into the
heart of affairs : every incident or dialogue, to
the closing page, follows without pause or digression, clear and firm as crystal. No trace of
obscurity or hesitation blurs the gay scene :
every character is vividly, and individually,

alive.   Yet how simple, almost commonplace, the material : how parochial the outlook. We have here no mystery or melodrama, no psychology or local colour.   Miss Austen's young ladies have absolutely no interests in life except " the men," however superior their manners and instincts to the egregious frivolity of Mrs. Bennet. They are the normal heroines of a conventional love-story ; with the usual surroundings—a handsome hero or two, some tiresome relatives, a confidante, a mild villain, and varied comic relief.   It has been said further that Miss Austen's ideal of a gentleman was deficient, since Darcy's insolence betrays lack of breeding : and, certainly, no Elizabeth of to-day would even temporarily be deceived or attracted by so common an adventurer as Wickham.

At a first glance, indeed, it might seem that Miss Austen depended entirely for her effects upon the creation of oddities.   Reflecting on Lady Catherine and Mr. Collins, touching perfection, we may well fancy that we have surprised her secret—the impulse of her achievement, the cause of our own enthusiasm.   This, however, is but a hasty and superficial impression.   To begin with, she does not concentrate, either in wit or humour, upon these figures of fun : and, in the second place, she has powers quite other than the mirth-provoking. Though grammatically not above reproach, she seems always to use the right word by instinct, hitting every nail full on the head, never wasting a syllable. The art nowhere obtrudes itself : her most skilfully polished phrases appear natural and fluent, just what her characters must have said in real life, to express precisely their thoughts and feelings. Faultlessly neat and compact, her style is yet daring, vigorous, and thoroughly alive.

Similar qualities appear in her delineation of character. Always knowing her own mind, and going straight to the point : there is no vagueness in outline, no uncertainty anywhere. Jane Bennet could never have said or done just what came most naturally from Elizabeth ; Darcy shared no thought or deed with his best friend : less prominent persons are as firmly, if less fully, individualised. The incidents, moreover, however trifling, are well varied ; the plot has ample movement—once those concerned in it have won our sympathies. Assuredly Miss Austen's aim is no strenuous ; but it is direct, vigorous, and clear-headed. And where she aims, she hits.

Sense and Sensibility reveals the very same method and the reappearance of many similar types, applied to an entirely new story in which no interest or situation repeats those of the earlier book. With her daring indifference to originality in the mechanical construction of a plot, Miss Austen once more centres her story round two sisters, more widely diverse in temperament, indeed, than Jane and Elizabeth, but no less everything to each other. Their mother, after the way of parents in these novels, is as foolish as Mrs. Bennet, though far more lovable. Willoughby is Wickham over again, with a fancy for accomplishments. The tragi-comedy introduced by Lucy Steele, more *essentially* vulgar than any of the Bennets, Mrs. Palmer's candid frivolity, and the languid elegance of Lady Middleton (later perfected in Lady Bertram), provide abundant occasion for laughter ; though no one figure of absurdity stands out so strongly as those of the earlier novel. On the other hand, Miss Austen has nowhere exposed a character more trenchantly by one short dialogue than in the discussion between Mr. and Mrs. John Dashwood about "what he could do for" his widowed mother and orphaned sisters. It were surely impossible for selfish hypocrisy to go further; and the subtle touches by which the wife reveals herself leader of the pair, must afford us the keenest enjoyment.

But this tale of Marianne and her Willoughby has one element entirely absent from *Pride and Prejudice*, and never again attempted by Jane Austen. It may be said to border on melodrama. The young people's ingenuous revels in emotion, whether of joy or grief, surprise one in so balanced a writer, and reveal powers we should not otherwise have suspected. Marianne, indeed, is the very personification of that sensibility, so dear to "elegant females" of the old world, so foreign to modern ideals. Having chosen her type, Miss Austen would seem determined to show how far she could go in this direction without distorting humanity. To the more conventional Miss Burney, sensibility was a grace essential in heroines. She is its acknowledged exponent, and compels us, despite prejudice, to recognise its real charm. But neither Evelina nor Cecilia exhibits so much naïveté as

Marianne, such tempestuous abandon, such a fiery glow ; yet we can read of her with equal patience, we can love her no less. She is saved, for us, by her genuine affection for " sensible " Eleanor, and her unselfish devotion to a mother who seems even younger and more foolish than herself. And Willoughby's temperament fits her like a glove. His wooing, his wickedness, and his repentance belong to a generation before Miss Austen's. Through this couple she triumphs in otherwise unexplored regions.

Northanger Abbey has very much the appearance of juvenile effort, possibly recast in maturity. If not actually written in girlhood, it must be regarded as the flower of a true holiday spirit, blossoming in sheer fun. Fresh from the excited perusal of some novel by the terrifying Anne Radcliffe, whom I believe Miss Austen enjoyed as keenly as her own Catherine, she must have thrown herself into the composition of this' delightful parody, just to renew its thrills, to linger over its absurdities. It is all pure farce, exaggeration cheerfully unrestrained. The irrepressible Arabella belongs to Miss Burney : her boasting brother should hang in the same

gallery.   Dear, foolish Catherine's idle imaginings about General Tilney were never meant to
resemble nature.   Henry could scarcely have
forgiven them, had he taken her quite seriously.
Moreover, having one parody in hand, Miss Austen
gaily embarks on yet another, no less irresponsible
and spontaneous.   Catherine is Evelina in miniature ; the real *ingénue* whose country breeding
exposes her to the most diverting distresses
in a Society amazingly mixed.   Hovering between Thorpes and Tilneys, like Evelina between
Mirvans and Branghtons, she enters each circle
with the same innocence, enthusiasm, and naïveté.
Miss Austen's sly boast of originality in allowing
her heroine to fall in love without stopping to
ascertain " the gentleman's feelings," is but gentle
raillery at a similar presumption in Miss Burney.
Certainly Orville, no less than Tilney, was led on
to serious thoughts of matrimony by the simple-
minded revelation of a pretty girl's partiality.

Where a laugh lurks behind every sentence, we
need not expect the special " studies in humour "
which stand out, everywhere, in the more serious
stories.   Yet General Tilney (later perfected in Sir
Walter Elliot) is a finished sketch : while John

Thorpe, who never opens his lips without betraying himself ; and Arabella, whether in pursuit of the " two young men " or quizzing the naughty Captain, were hard to beat.

Nowhere, in all her work, has Miss Austen concentrated such pungent sarcasm as in the condescending explanation of how much folly reasonable men *prefer* in lovely women.

" The advantages of natural folly in a beautiful girl have been already set forth by the capital pen of a sister author ; and to her treatment of the subject I will only add, in justice to men, that though to the larger and more trifling part of the sex, imbecility in females is a great enhancement of their personal charms, there is a portion of them too reasonable, and too well informed themselves, to desire anything more in woman than ignorance."

Do not the smooth words sting ?

Approaching the second group, we look naturally, and not in vain, for evidence of maturity and development. Miss Austen does not, in fact, make any attempt to enlarge her sphere, to widen her outlook, to handle more strenuous emotion. But her plots, still based on parochial gossip, are more varied and complex : she works with a larger number of characters ; actually perfecting

some types already familiar, and introducing us
to many a new acquaintance. Above all, her
dramatis personæ are no longer fixed and defined
at their first entrance : they grow with the story,
often surprising us at last by qualities, no doubt
dormant from the beginning, and never strained
or inconsistent, but only possible to development
through experience.

Emma obviously invites comparison with *Pride
and Prejudice.* The two heroines have long shared
almost equally the position of a most popular
favourite : one or other of the two books is almost
universally judged her best. The charms of Emma
and Harriet are more *naturally* diverse because
they are *not* sisters : yet in the accidents of inti-
macy, mutual confidence, and common interests
they form a basis for the plot precisely similar to
that of the sisters in *Pride and Prejudice* or *Sense
and Sensibility*, not greatly differing from those in
Mansfield Park or *Persuasion.* Mr. Elton, the
very pink of pretentious vulgarity, recalls Lydia
and Lucy Steele : her *caro sposo* eclipses Mr. Collins
on his own ground. Miss Bates the garrulous,
and Mr. Woodhouse the fussy, varied examples of
the eternal bore, are formidable rivals, if not

conquerors, of the inimitable Lady Catherine.
Here we have " characters " in greater abundance,
almost more finished in fuller detail.

Advance is more obvious, however, in the introduction of such independent family groups as the
Westons, the Martins, the John Knightleys, and the
Eltons : in the presence of a full-grown secondary
plot—" The Fairfax Mystery," as we might call it :
and in the heroine's *development* through experience.
A secret engagement is, in itself, new kind of
material for Jane Austen to handle : well calculated to exercise her delicate command of dialogue.
It lends particular interest to this novel, however
simple the intrigue compared with more modern
examples, however foreign to our own conceptions
the " sense of sin " thereby engendered in Jane
Fairfax. Young Churchill's spirited conduct of
the affair is a perpetual delight, certainly not least
for its unintentional humbling of " the great Miss
Woodhouse " : though his insinuations about Mr.
Dixon (like Darcy's rudeness) exceed the licence
permitted a gentleman, however spoilt and high-
spirited.

We have already noted the popularity of Emma,
but, in this *unlike* Elizabeth, she has her detractors.

Some find her too managing, self-centred, and
" superior " for charm.   Admittedly she is a match-
maker, far less refined than she imagines herself :
her rudeness to Miss Bates is difficult to pardon.
But, as Knightley alone had the wit to recognise,
Harriet's innocent folly encouraged her worst
qualities, and Emma's repentance is sincere, bearing
good fruit.   To the end she is herself indeed ; but
how different a self—standing witness to the
powers of character in bringing out the best of us.
Having played with fire, she learnt her lesson, and
so we may leave her, no less marvelling than she
at the workings of what little Harriet was pleased
to call her heart ; admiring, as all must, Jane
Austen's finished study of that engaging " Miss."

Mansfield Park, probably, is the least popular
of the novels—on account of its heroine.   Fanny
Price has her partisans, but can never become a
general favourite, until we again idealise humility
in woman.   Accepting, without a murmur, the
most unreasonable and most exacting demands of
all her " betters " ; meekly grateful, to the point of
servility, if Edmund bestows on her a kind word ;
she stands before us condemned by every code
accepted to-day.

Yet Fanny, reversing the process in Emma, acquires self-confidence with years, and actually learns to play the heroine in adversity. The novel contains Miss Austen's first, and last, picture of the great world beyond parish boundaries : it deals, successfully, with greater contrasts in social status than she ever attempted before or since. Lady Bertram, no less than Mrs. Norris, fairly eclipses all former achievements in character study.

Its crowded canvas, indeed, demands notice in detail. Sir Thomas neglects his family much as did Mr. Bennet, and suffers more serious punishment. The " villain " is replaced by Henry and Miss Crawford, of the world, worldly : figuring at first as very wholesome instruments of distraction to a stiff family circle ; but ingeniously convicted, in touch with realities, of serious moral depravity. Their presence, however, reveals new power in the authoress, and considerably enlivens the scene. They do much towards the development of Fanny.·

No two characters, on the other hand, could be more profoundly diverse than those of Lady Bertram and Mrs. Norris : yet they fit each other without friction, and it were hard indeed to say which is more perfectly drawn. A woman more

utterly devoid of feeling or lacking in common
sense than the former, it is impossible to conceive.
The mere hint of responsibility towards anyone or
anything would have shattered her nerves completely ; and no emergency, of joy or grief, ever
taught her to face the exertion of making up
her own mind for herself on the most trivial
question. Yet there is no exaggeration. She
is perfectly natural, not without charm, an ornament to the family circle whom all would miss.
For Mrs. Norris, the intolerable busybody, it
has been suggested that Miss Austen owed something directly to personal experience. Was this
her revenge for much silent endurance ? Certainly so much concentrated scorn, so stern a
portrait seems to imply animus. Gentle, tender,
and sympathetic by nature, was she at times
lashed to fury by the cruel inanity of village
types ? Mrs. Elton, Miss Bates, and Mr. Collins
may, in a less degree, have been similarly inspired.
If it be so, verily they have their reward.

The central motive in *Mansfield Park* is
more complex than heretofore : its scenes more
varied. The whole episode of Fanny's visit to
her struggling parents, and their squalid home,

introduces an aspect of life elsewhere ignored, shows us humanity unrefined. The work is alive and vigorous, not altogether foreign to modern realism. Coming, moreover, from such uncongenial, and to them unfamiliar, surroundings; bred to hard work and hard times; cousin Fanny brings a new element into the lives of the elegant Miss Bertrams, our usual couple of sisters; who, again, are destined to further awakening from the manners and experience of Mary Crawford.

Finally, we have here the nearest approach to a so-called " social problem " ever handled by Jane Austen, and a thoroughly serious picture of punishment. It may seem hard to all of us, and modern casuists would certainly declare it unjust, that Maria should suffer so much more than Julia, who had no more principle, but less opportunity. In this matter, however, Miss Austen is uncompromising. Of the two Maria was more spoilt—by Mrs. Norris, more exposed to temptation; and actually committed sin. *Therefore she must expect punishment.* Julia proved herself equally cold-hearted and selfish; but by luck, neither through wisdom nor goodness, she kept within the code—and was forgiven.

Miss Austen does not let off the man altogether ;
for it is quite clear that Henry Crawford lost Fanny,
and, with her, his best chance for happiness. But
Maria lost everything ; and so, the authoress seems
to imply, it must be always. There is no hint
of mercy, no chance for retrievement, in one of
the sternest decrees of Fate that could overtake
a woman — perpetual imprisonment with her
aunt !

"Shut up together with little society, on one side
no affection, on the other no judgment, it may reasonably be supposed that their tempers became their
mutual punishment."

Justice, indeed, hath fair play with Mrs. Norris.
May we not whisper—Poor Maria !

Persuasion, Miss Austen's last work and perhaps her finest, reveals maturity in other ways.
No longer than *Northanger Abbey*, it has neither
the complexity nor the crowded canvas distinguishing others of the second group. It is
written throughout in a minor key, without one
outstanding comic " character." But, on the
other hand, its construction is singularly compact, its emotions have a new depth, sincerity,
and tenderness. Anne Elliot can never rival

Elizabeth or Emma; though she is no less
" superior " to her own family, and has in reality
more character. Here our appreciation and our
sympathies are emotional rather than intellectual.
We feel with her far more than with them. Though
never recognised in her own circle, as were all
Miss Austen's heroines save Fanny Price, she
dominates the story more than any. *Persuasion*,
in fact, is a study in character, such as its
authoress had never before attempted. No more,
if indeed actually less, sensational than its predecessors, the whole scheme moves below the
surface. It holds us more by feeling and atmosphere than by incident. We experience a similar
delight in the perfectly turned phrases, the finished
dialogue, and the neat characterisation; but
here are no figures of fun, no animated social
functions, no clash of types. We may smile,
indeed, at Sir Walter Elliot or at the family of
Uppercross; but the humour, however subtle
and permeating, does not anywhere prevail over
deeper emotion.

Certainly we note that Miss Austen still seeks
out no new material, depends on no more startling
situation. Anne's happiness and misery alike

arise, as did Jane's and Elizabeth's, from a refinement to which every other member of her family
was absolutely blind. The natural understanding between two sisters is destroyed, as between
Julia and Maria, by rivalry for the one eligible
visitor to the neighbourhood ; though here with
no permanently disastrous results. The naïvely
conceived villain of the first group has become
—again as in *Mansfield Park*—an accomplished
man of the world, with no sister indeed to further
his perfectly honourable designs on the heroine,
but, in the last event, not lacking a female
accomplice. Its most striking effect in local
colour, the glowing picture of naval types,
was foreshadowed in William Price : though
Admiral and Mrs. Croft admittedly stand high
in Miss Austen's gallery of character-studies.
Society, as in *Northanger Abbey*, is located at
Bath.

Yet nowhere has she attempted, with any approach to a like depth of feeling or earnestness,
so much philosophy on life, so searching an
analysis of human nature, as in the remarkable
conversation on faithfulness, as severally exhibited by men and women, which artistically

produces a permanent understanding between
hero and heroine.

"Oh!" cried Anne eagerly to Captain Harville, "I
hope I do justice to all that is felt by you and by those
who resemble you. God forbid that I should under-
value the warm and faithful feelings of any of my
fellow-creatures. I should deserve utter contempt if
I dared to suppose that true attachment and constancy
were known only by woman. No, I believe you capable
of everything great and good in your married lives. I
believe you equal to every important exertion, and to
every domestic forbearance, so long as—if I may be
allowed the expression—so long as you have an object.
I mean while the woman you love lives, and lives for
you. All the privilege I claim for my own sex (it is
not a very enviable one : you need not covet it) is
that of loving longest, when existence or when hope
is gone."

This is the text of the whole novel, woven
with subtlety into its very fabric, inspiring each
thought, each word, though never obtruding.
Persuasion is neither a sermon nor a pamphlet.
Its author assuredly holds no brief for woman,
brings no charge against man. Yet here she
speaks for her sex. Of what she has seen and
felt it would appear that she could no longer
remain silent.

Jane Austen reveals herself in her last message to posterity.

Sense and Sensibility, 1811.
Pride and Prejudice, 1813.
Mansfield Park, 1814.
Emma, 1816.
Northanger Abbey, 1818.
Persuasion, 1818.

A "MOST ACCOMPLISHED COQUETTE"

IN spite of the almost universal inclination to pass over Jane Austen's " minor " works without serious comment, we are ourselves strongly disposed to consider *Lady Susan* of considerable importance.

The early compositions, if sprightly, are not precocious : the cancelled chapter of *Persuasion*— replaced only eleven months before her death by chaps. x. and xi.—remains an interesting record of what would have fully satisfied a less careful artist ; and the description—with extracts—which Mr. Austen-Leigh has given us of the novel begun on 27th January 1817 and continued until the 17th of March,[1] does not contain body enough for confident anticipation : *i.e.* of detail. There is, however, no reason for dreading any decline in artistic power.

Water-marks of 1803 and 1804 on the original manuscript prove *The Watsons* to have been written

---

[1] She died 18th July 1817.

H

between her two periods of productive activity ;
and it is not likely that definite evidence will now
transpire in explanation of its having been left
unfinished : unless we accept Mr. Austen-Leigh's
somewhat fastidious conclusion—

"that the author became aware of the evil of having
placed her heroine too low, in such a position of poverty
and obscurity as, though not necessarily connected
with vulgarity, has a sad tendency to degenerate
into it ; and therefore, like a singer who has begun on
too low a note, she discontinued the strain. It was an
error of which she was likely to become more sensible,
as she grew older, and saw more of society : certainly
she never repeated it by placing the heroine of any
subsequent work under circumstances likely to be
unfavourable to the refinement of a lady." [1]

Her nephew further remarks that " it could not
have been broken up for the purpose of using the
materials in another fabric " ; although, in his
opinion, a resemblance between Mr. Robert Watson
and Mr. Elton is " very discernible." We might
also observe that Mr. Watson appears to have taken
his " basin of gruel " as regularly as Mr. Woodhouse ; while, on the other hand, Lord Osborne's
affected superiority to dancing recalls Darcy. Miss

[1] It may surely be questioned whether this remark quite
allows for the home of Fanny Price.

Watson's theories on life and marriage are particularly characteristic :

"I would rather do anything than be a teacher at a school. *I* have been at school, Emma, and know what a life they lead ; *you* never have. I should not like marrying a disagreeable man any more than yourself ; but I do not think there *are* many very disagreeable men ; I think I could like any good-humoured man with a comfortable income. I suppose my aunt brought you up to be rather refined."

Emma Watson, in fact, like all Jane Austen's heroines, shines by *comparison* with the rest of her family.

Lady Susan, unlike any of the stories mentioned above, is obviously complete and finished. "Her family have always believed it to be an early production"; but we cannot conjecture why it was laid aside and never published by her. It is, however, an "experiment"—never repeated ; and very possibly Jane Austen did not feel moved to revise what evidently had not satisfied her own standard of perfection.

For us, however, its striking dissimilarity to the six recognised "works," and its unique position in the development of fiction, are of peculiar interest. To begin with, it belongs to the old "picaresque" school of fiction, seldom popular in England, though practised with considerable vigour by Defoe, and *once* revived by Thackeray in a work of genius— *Barry Lyndon*.

It may, perhaps, be considered an exaggeration to call the heroine a villain ; and certainly Jane Austen entirely avoids the sordid material of criminal adventure (*not* scorned by Thackeray) ; which is the recognised foundation of ordinary picaresque work. But the essential characteristic remains prominent. The good people are comparatively colourless ; our interest centres around *Lady Susan*, and it is on her that the author has devoted her most careful work. Moreover, it should not be overlooked that *Lady Susan* does contemplate, and actually instigate—in refined language—a course of action which may fairly be called criminal. The confidante, Mrs. Johnson— a recognised appendage to villainy—receives the following significant hint :

" Mainwaring is more devoted o me than ever ; and were we at liberty, I doubt if I could resist even matrimony offered by *him*. This event, if his wife live with you, it may be in your power to hasten. The violence of her feelings, which must wear her out, may easily be kept in irritation. *I rely on your friendship for this.*"

The quiet audacity of this paragraph is really astounding; and just because no other word in all the forty-one letters contains so much as a hint at anything beyond unblushing effrontery and reckless lying, we regard it, without hesitation, as the keynote of Jane Austen's method, and the declaration of her aim. Only a villain could possibly have written these words; only a genius could have refrained from giving her away on some other occasion.

Superficially, Lady Susan is no worse than a merry widow, given to man conquest, perfectly indifferent—if not contemptuous—towards the wives or the fiancées of her victims. In this matter, indeed, her enemies complain that " she does not confine herself to that sort of honest flirtation which satisfies most people, but aspires to the more delicious gratification of making a whole family miserable." During the first months of widowhood she had determined on " discretion "; and being " as quiet as possible " :—" I have admitted no one's attentions but Mainwaring's. I have avoided *all general flirtation* whatever; I have distinguished no creature besides, of all the numbers resorting hither, except Sir John Martin,

on whom I bestowed a little notice, in order to
detach him from Miss Mainwaring ; but, if the
world could know my motive *there* they would
honour me " ;—the fact being that she wanted
the man for her daughter.

This " most accomplished coquette in England "
is described with some fullness by a sister-in-law
who had every reason to think ill of her.

" She is really excessively pretty ; however you
may choose to question the allurements of a lady no
longer young, I must, for my own part, declare that
I have seldom seen so lovely a woman as Lady Susan.
She is delicately fair, with fine grey eyes and dark
eyelashes ; and from her appearance one would not
suppose her more than five and twenty ; though she
must in fact be ten years older. I was certainly not
disposed to admire her, though always hearing she
was beautiful ; but I cannot help feeling that she
possesses an uncommon union of symmetry, brilliancy,
and grace. Her address to me was so gentle, frank,
and even affectionate, that, if I had not known how
much she has always disliked me for marrying Mr.
Vernon, and that we had never met before, I should
have imagined her an attached friend. One is apt, I
believe, to connect assurance of manner with coquetry,
and to expect that an impudent address will naturally
attend an impudent mind ; at least, I myself was
prepared for an improper degree of confidence in Lady
Susan : but her countenance is absolutely sweet, and

her voice and manner winningly mild. I am sorry it
is so, for what is this but deceit ? Unfortunately, one
knows her too well. She is clever and agreeable, has
all that knowledge of the world which makes conversation easy, and talks very well, with a happy
command of language, which is too often used, I believe,
to make black appear white."

Such being the lady's own manners and sentiments, we are fully prepared for her satirical
references to her daughter :

" I never saw a girl of her age "—she was sixteen—
" bid fairer to be the sport of mankind. Her feelings
are tolerably acute, and she is so charmingly artless in
their display as to afford the most reasonable hope of
her being ridiculous, and despised by every man who
sees her. Artlessness will never do in love-matters ;
and that girl is born a simpleton who has it either by
nature or affectation."

It is hardly necessary to add that Lady Susan
has no desire, or ambition, in life beyond universal
admiration. She is " tempted " indeed, but does
not on one occasion lose her head : and we cannot
feel that she was even exactly pre-eminent in
her practice. It does not appear that she quite
succeeded in ever enjoying the fruits of victory.
Miss Austen has not drawn for us a really " cunning " coquette. Lady Susan subdued men, but

she could seldom hold them ; and on no occasion does she conquer " circumstances," *i.e.*, other women.

There may be, obviously, three explanations of this fact. Either Jane Austen was lacking in the more robust humour of Thackeray and his predecessors, who seem to revel in the gaiety of the heartless ; or she recognised the limitations of country life, where the artificial can never prosper for long ; or she had, in her own quiet way, too much principle to countenance, even in fiction, any permanent happiness for the wicked.

However it be, the result is unique. Lady Susan stands alone as a heroine. As we have seen, the full depths of her criminality lurk beneath the surface : her power is rather hinted at than described. It is only on looking back over the accumulation of slight touches and chance words that we realise her astounding insincerity, her absolute lack of feeling, or the brilliance of her superficial attractiveness. It is a very short book, containing few characters and practically no events ; yet we are startled, on reflection, at its unsparing picture of the incalculable amount of mischief that may be done by sheer empty-headedness, entirely without strong feeling or passion ; and of the incredible isolation in which such a character must always live.

Lady Susan injures, in some degree, literally every person named in the whole story. She has not a friend in the world. In reality, perhaps, the last consideration indicates most clearly the virtue in Miss Austen's characterisation. It is not once even mentioned, and, consequently, arouses no remark. We must deduct from it our own observation. But, inasmuch as never for one instant does a single thought for anyone but herself cross the mind of Lady Susan, so never does anyone else show one spark of affection for her. Mrs. Johnson, obviously, was governed by interested motives, and frankly abandons her at the first serious danger of " the consequences " to herself. The kind of devotion she inspired in men had no affinity to friendship, respect, consideration, or unselfishness. The closing scene is described with a cutting brevity, that recalls Miss Austen's dismissal of Maria Rushworth and Mrs. Norris.

She married the man designed for her daughter— for an establishment : " Whether Lady Susan was or was not happy in her second choice, I do not see how it can ever be ascertained ; for who would take her assurance of it on either side of the question ? The world must judge from probabilities ; she had nothing against her but her husband, and her conscience."

As we have noticed before, Miss Austen seldom obtrudes her opinions, but they are occasionally implied. And, on such occasions, they are unhesitating. We find in her no doubt, no compromise —we might almost say no charity—about a few questions of ultimate morality.

On the whole, however, we cannot claim for *Lady Susan* all those perfections of style associated with the genius of its author. Save for a few turns of phrase, of which we have quoted the most significant, it has little of her pointed epigram or subtle humour. The language is equally finished and inevitable, but there is neither sparkle nor gaiety. We miss the dialogue and the delicate variety in characterisation. It would be hazardous, indeed, to suppose that anyone could have " discovered " Jane Austen from Lady Susan ; but, knowing her other work, we can detect the mastery.

In conclusion, it is worth noticing that she has

here given us some insight into the constancy of man.

Reginald de Courcy had been a victim of Lady Susan's. After her second marriage, her daughter

" Frederika was fixed in the family of her uncle and aunt till such time as Reginald de Courcy could be talked, flattered, and finessed into an affection for her which, allowing leisure for the conquest of his attachment to her mother, for his abjuring all future attachments, and detesting the sex, *might be reasonably looked for in a twelvemonth.* Three months might have done it in general, but Reginald's feelings were no less lasting than lively."

It will be remembered that Miss Austen is less explicit about Edmund Bertram :

" I purposely abstain from dates on this occasion, that every one may be at liberty to fix their own, aware that the cure of unconquerable passions, and the transfer of unchanging attachments, must vary much as to time in different people. I only entreat everybody to believe that exactly at the time when it was quite natural that it should be so, and not a week earlier, Edmund did cease to care about Miss Crawford, and became as anxious to marry Fanny as Fanny herself could desire."

On the other hand, Marianne Dashwood required

two years to conquer her devotion to Willoughby in favour of Colonel Brandon ; but then Miss Austen has claimed for her sex, through Anne Elliot, " the privilege of loving longest, when existence, or when hope, is gone."

PARALLEL PASSAGES

It would be difficult, if not impossible, to name an author of genius even approximately equal to Jane Austen's who owed so little as she to any deliberate study of literary models or conscious attention to the laws of style. Concerning her personal character and private interests we know, indeed, surprisingly little ; but it is certain, on the one hand, that she was not in touch with the men and women of letters among her contemporaries, and, on the other, that her family circle did not practise the gentle art of criticism. The further assumption that she had thought little, and read less, about the theory of her art, is justified by the absence of any such references in her letters, and by her simple ideas of construction, as developed in the advice to a young relative who was attempting to follow her example :

" You are now collecting your people delightfully, getting them exactly into such a spot as is the delight of my life. Three or four families in a country village is the very thing to work on."

Jane Austen, however, read novels with keen enjoyment : *Northanger Abbey* is in part an avowed burlesque of Mrs. Radcliffe, and we can discover, in the language of Shakespearean commentary, the " originals " for several of her plots and persons in the works of Fanny Burney.

Such an investigation, indeed, seems to have been almost courted by the author herself when she borrowed a title from a chance phrase of her sister-novelist's, for a story with a somewhat similar plot, developed, among other coincidences, in two closely parallel scenes. When at length, after a series of cruel misfortunes, the hero and heroine of *Cecilia* were permitted to console each other, an onlooker thus pointed the moral of their experience : " The whole of this unfortunate business has been the result of PRIDE AND PREJUDICE."

There must have been a day, about twenty years after they were written, when these words assumed, in Jane Austen's eyes, a sudden significance. She had read them before, probably many times, but on this occasion they proved no less than an inspiration. Within her desk, on which perhaps the favourite volume was then lying, lay the neatly written manuscript of a tale constructed, in some measure, on the lines of this very *Cecilia*. She had called it *First Impressions*. Would not *Pride and Prejudice* be a better name? It was certainly a happy thought.[1]

Now Delvile, like Darcy, fell in love against his family instincts, and, with an equally offensive condescension, discoursed at length on his struggles between pride and passion to the young lady he desired to honour with his affection. He, too, resisted long, yielded in the end, and was forgiven. His mother's appeal to Cecilia was as violent, and almost as impertinent, as Lady Catherine's to Elizabeth.

A close comparison of these two parallel scenes will serve at once to show Jane Austen's familiarity with the copy and her originality of treatment. Darcy, like Delvile, is not " more eloquent on the subject of tenderness than of pride." But he has overcome his scruples and offers his hand, in confidence of its being accepted, to one who dislikes and despises him. Delvile, on the other hand,

---

[1] There is good ground for thinking that the change of title was made after the novel was finished, for Mr. Austen-Leigh says that *Pride and Prejudice* was written between October 1796 and August 1797, while it is referred to as *First Impressions* in letters as late as June 1799.

wishes merely to explain the reasons that have
induced him to deny himself the dangerous solace
of the " society " of one whom he believes to be
entirely indifferent to him, and to excuse the
occasional outbursts of tenderness into which he
has been betrayed in unguarded moments.   He does
not complain of " the inferiority of her connections,"
but of the clause in her uncle's will by which her
future husband is compelled to take her name.
Cecilia had been puzzled by his uncertain behaviour,
but, believing him only cautious from respect to his
parents, had permitted herself to love him.

Mrs. Delvile again, like Lady Catherine, based
her appeal on the " honour and credit " of the
young man she was so anxious to release ; but her
insolence was tempered by affection, and disguised
by high-sounding moral sentiments. Cecilia was
softened, as Elizabeth had not been, by a sense of
gratitude for past kindness and by a strained notion
of respect for the older lady. Mrs. Delvile, except
in her pride, is intended to inspire us with genuine
respect ; Lady Catherine is always treated with
amused contempt.

There are other instances—less familiar, but
equally striking—in which Miss Austen made

use, in her own inimitable fashion, of characters, phrases, and situations in *Evelina* and *Cecilia*.

Mr. Delvile, the pompous and foolish man of family, reappears in Sir Walter Elliot of *Persuasion*, and General Tilney of *Northanger Abbey*. Cecilia could never determine "whether Mr. Delvile's haughtiness or his condescension humbled her most," and he became "at length so infinitely condescending, with intention to give her courage, that he totally depressed her with mortification and chagrin." Catherine Morland always found that "in spite of General Tilney's great civilities to her, in spite of his thanks, invitations, and compliments, it had been a release to get away from him."

Cecilia's friendship for Henrietta Belfield resembles Emma's for Harriet Smith. She was ever watching the state of her young friend's heart ; now soliciting her confidence, and again, from motives of prudence, rejecting it. For a time both girls are in love with the hero, and Henrietta dreams as fondly and as foolishly over Delvile's imagined partiality as Harriet did over Knightley's. Neither heroine has any thought of resigning her lover to her friend, or "of resolving to refuse him at once and for ever, without vouch-safing any motive, because he could not marry them both."

The following conversation between Mr. Gosport and Miss Larolles recalls Miss Steele's persistence in laughing at herself about the doctor (*Sense and Sensibility*), and Tom Bertram's affected belief that Miss Crawford was " quizzing him and Miss Anderson " (*Mansfield Park*).

Gosport attacks Miss Larolles on a rumour now current about her, and, after some skirmish-ing, confesses to having heard that " she had left off talking."

" ' Oh, was that all,' cried she, disappointed. ' I thought it had been something about Mr. Sawyer, for I declare I have been plagued so about him, I am quite sick of his name.'

" ' And for my part, I never heard it ! So fear nothing from me on his account.'

" ' Lord, Mr. Gosport, how can you say so ! I am sure you must know about the festino that night, for it was all over the town in a moment.'

" ' What festino ? '

" ' Well, only conceive how provoking ! Why, I know nothing else was talked of for a month.' "

This is the Miss Larolles who haunted the mind of Anne Elliot, in *Persuasion*, when she moved to the end of a form at the concert, in order to be sure of not missing Captain Wentworth :

" She could not do so without comparing herself with Miss Larolles, the inimitable Miss Larolles, but still she did it, and not with much happier effect."

Here is the passage in question : " Do you know," says Miss Larolles,

" Mr. Meadows has not spoke one word to me all the evening ! though I am sure he saw me, for *I sat at the outside* on purpose to speak to a person or two, that I knew would be strolling about ; for if one sits on the inside there's no speaking to a creature you know ; so I never do it at the opera, nor in the boxes at Ranelagh, nor anywhere. It's the shockingest thing you can conceive, to be made sit in the middle of these forms, one might as well be at home, for nobody can speak to one."

The singularly unselfish affection of Mrs. and Miss Mirvan for Evelina, never clouded by envy of her superior attractions, finds its echo in the experience of Jane Fairfax :

" The affection of the whole family, the warm attachment of Miss Campbell in particular, was the more honourable to each party, from the circumstance of Jane's decided superiority, both in beauty and acquirements."

When Evelina is in great trouble, and the " best

of men," Mr. Villars, is penetrated to the heart
by the sight of her grief, he can think of no better
consolation than :

"My dearest child, I cannot bear to see thy tears ;
for my sake dry them : such a sight is too much for
me : *think of that*, Evelina, and take comfort, I charge
thee."

With similar masculine futility the self-centred
Edmund Bertram attempts to soften the grief
of his dear cousin :

"No wonder—you must feel it—you must suffer.
How a man who had once loved, could desert you
But yours—your regard was new compared with——
Fanny, *think of me*."

Many a reader, doubtless, has, with Elizabeth
Bennet, "lifted up his eyes in amazement" at
the platitudes of Mary on the occasion of Lydia's
elopement, without suspecting that offensive
young moralist of having culled her phrases
from the earlier novelist. "Remember, my
dear Evelina," writes Mr. Villars, "nothing is
so delicate as the reputation of a woman; *it is
at once the most beautiful and most brittle* of all
human things." Now Mary was "a great reader
and made extracts." She evidently studied the

art of judicious quotation : " Unhappy as the
event must be for Lydia," says this astounding
sister,

" we may draw from it this useful lesson : that loss
of virtue in a female is irretrievable—that one false
step involves her in endless ruin—that her reputation
is no less brittle than it is beautiful, and that she cannot
be too guarded in her behaviour towards the unde-
serving of the other sex."

The general resemblance of Catherine Morland's
situation to Evelina's may have been unconscious,
but was scarcely, we think, accidental. In
Northanger Abbey, as in no other of Miss Austen's
novels, though in all Miss Burney's, the heroine
is detached from her ordinary surroundings and
introduced to society under the inefficient protection of foolish acquaintances. Like Evelina,
she finds in the great world much cause for alarm
and anxiety, though, like her, she has the hero for
partner at her first ball. She, too, is frequently
tormented by the differences between her aristo-
cratic and her vulgar friends. Henry Tilney's
attitude towards her, on the other hand, is very
similar to Lord Orville's towards Evelina. He can
read her like an open book, and his discovery of

her suspicions about his father is as ingenious and as delicately revealed as Orville's generous chivalry to Evelina at the ridotto. Indeed, had Fanny Burney been more daring she would have confessed that Orville's affection for Evelina, like Tilney's for Catherine,

" originated in nothing better than gratitude ; or in other words, that a persuasion of her partiality for him had been the only cause of giving her a serious thought."

The admiration which Evelina expressed with so much naïveté and earnestness to her guardian must have betrayed itself in her looks and conversation. Orville's heart was won by unconscious flattery, though Miss Burney herself was too conventional to admit it. She left the conception and its defence to another. " It is a new circumstance in romance," writes Miss Austen, " and dreadfully derogatory of an heroine's dignity ; but if it be as new in common life, the credit of a wild imagination will at least be all my own."

We can scarcely avoid wondering whether Miss Austen remembered Sir Clement Willoughby when she decided upon the name of Marianne's devoted, but faithless, lover. The two men bear somewhat similar relations to hero and heroine.

In one of her rare outbursts of self-confidence
with the reader, Miss Austen appears to put *Camilla*
on a level with *Cecilia* ; and Thorpe's abuse of this
novel in *Northanger Abbey* must be interpreted as
her own indirect praise, for that youth is never
allowed to open his lips without exposing himself
to our derision. It is immaterial to our purpose
that posterity has accepted his verdict rather than
Miss Austen's. Her name appears among the
subscribers to *Camilla,* and she was loyal to it
without an effort. Here she was not likely to
find much available material ; but the conduct
of Miss Margland towards Sir Hugh Tyrold and
his adopted children may have suggested some
traits in Mrs. Norris, and Mr. Westwyn's naïve
enthusiasm for his son bears a strong resemblance
to that of Mr. Weston[1] for the inevitable Frank
Churchill.

Miss Bingley made herself ridiculous by her
definition of an accomplished woman as one who
" must have a thorough knowledge of music,
singing, drawing, dancing, and the modern languages." The germ of the satire appears in the
experiences of Miss Burney's *The Wanderer,* and

---

[1] Even the names here sound unexpectedly similar.

in an allusion to the prevalent idea of feminine culture in *Camilla* :

" A little music, a little drawing, and a little dancing, which should all be but slightly pursued, to distinguish a lady of fashion from an artist."

So writes Jane Austen, again, in *Lady Susan* :

" Not that I am an advocate for the prevailing fashion of acquiring a perfect knowledge of all languages, arts, and sciences. It is throwing away time to be mistress of French, Italian, and German ; music, singing, and dancing. . . . I do not mean, therefore, that Frederika's acquirements should be more than superficial, and I flatter myself that she will not ɪemain long enough at school to understand anything thoroughly."

It remains only to notice with what kindred indignation the two writers complain of the little honour accorded their craft. Miss Burney, in fact, did much to raise her profession ; but it was not considered " quite respectable " by Miss Austen's contemporaries.

Mr. Delvile complains of Cecilia's large bill at the booksellers', on the ground that

" a lady, whether so called from birth, or only from fortune, should never degrade herself by being put on a level with writers, and such sort of people."

In the preface to *Evelina* Miss Burney declares that

" in the republic of letters, there is no member of such inferior rank, or who is so much disdained by his brethren of the quill, as the humble novelist ; nor is his fate less hard in the world at large, since, among the whole class of writers, perhaps not one can be named of which the votaries are more numerous but less respectable."

Jane Austen is more spirited in her complaint, and takes her example from Miss Burney herself :

" Yes, novels ; for I will not adopt that ungenerous and impolitic custom, so common with novel-writers, of degrading, by their contemptuous censure, the very performances to the number of which they are themselves adding ; joining with their greatest enemies in bestowing the harshest epithets on such works, and scarcely ever permitting them to be read by their own heroine, who, if she accidentally take up a novel, is sure to turn over its insipid pages with disgust. Alas ! if the heroine of one novel be not patronised by the heroine of another, from whom can she expect protection and regard ? I cannot approve it. Let us leave it to the Reviewers to abuse such effusions of fancy at their leisure, and over every new novel to talk in threadbare strains of the trash with which the Press now groans. Let us not desert one another ; we are an injured body. Although our productions have afforded more extensive and unaffected pleasure than those of any other literary corporation in the world, no species of composition has been so much decried. From pride, ignorance, or fashion, our foes are almost as many as our readers ; and while the ability of the nine-hundredth abridger of the History of England, or of the man who collects and publishes in a volume some dozen lines of Milton, Pope, and Prior, with a paper from the *Spectator* and a chapter from Sterne, is eulogised by a thousand pens, there seems almost a general wish of decrying the capacity and undervaluing the labour of the novelist, and of slighting the performances which have only genius, wit, and taste to recommend them. ' I am no novel-reader ; I seldom look into novels ; it is really very well for a novel.' Such is the common cant. ' And what are you reading, Miss —— ? ' ' Oh, it's only a novel ! ' replies the young lady, while she lays down her book with affected indifference or momentary shame. ' It is only *Cecilia*, or *Camilla*, or *Belinda*,' or, in short, only some work in which the greatest powers of mind are displayed, in which the most thorough knowledge of human nature, the happiest delineation of its varieties, the liveliest effusions of wit and humour, are conveyed to the world in the best chosen language."

"PERSUASION" TO "JANE EYRE"

(1818–1847)

SUSAN FERRIER (1782–1854) once declared that
" perhaps, after all, the only uncloying pleasure in
life is that of fault-finding " ; and this cynical conclusion may serve to measure, in some degree, the
peculiar flavour of her brisk satire. The fact is,
that she acquired her notions of literary skill from
intimate association with " the Modern Athens,"
as Edinburgh then styled itself, wherein " Crusty
Christopher " and " The Ploughman Poet " held
sway. It was here, as we know, that "Brougham and
his confederates " formed that conspiracy of scorn,
The Edinburgh Review, which Wilson out-Heroded in
Blackwood. Following Miss Burney, in her spirited
exhibition of " Humours," Miss Ferrier also continued the Edgeworth " national " novel, by exploit-
ing a period of Scotch history untouched by Scott.
As her friend, Wilson, remarks in the *Noctes* :

" These novels have one feature of true and melancholy interest quite peculiar to themselves. It is in

them alone that the ultimate breaking-down and de-
basement of the Highland character has been depicted.
Sir Walter Scott had fixed the enamel of genius over
the last fitful flames of their half-savage chivalry, but
a humbler and sadder scene—the age of lucre-banished
clans—of chieftains dwindled into imitation squires,
and of chiefs content to barter the recollections of a
thousand years for a few gaudy seasons of Almacks
and Crockfords, the euthanasia of kilted aldermen and
steamboat pibrochs was reserved for Miss Ferrier."

And for the accuracy of her picture, the authoress
herself lays claim to having paid careful attention
to the results of deliberate study. " You may
laugh," she writes to Miss Clavering, " at the idea
of its being at all necessary for the writer of a
romance to be versed in the history, natural and
political, the modes, manners, customs, etc., of
the country where its bold and wanton freaks
are to be played ; but I consider it most essentially
so, as nothing disgusts even an ordinary reader
more than a discovery of the ignorance of the
author, who is pretending to instruct and amuse."

Meanwhile, the " Highlander " was more or less
in fashion, and Susan Ferrier set off her picture by
vivid contrasts with the most *recherché* daughters
of Society. An elegant slave of passion longs to fly
with her Henry to the desert—" a beautiful place,

full of roses and myrtles, and smooth, green turf,
and murmuring rivulets, and though very retired,
not absolutely out of the world ; where one could
occasionally see one's friends, and give *déjeuner et
fêtes-champêtres.*" So the foolish Indiana in Miss
Burney's *Camilla* considered a " cottage " but
" as a bower of eglantine and roses, where she
might repose and be adored all day long."

But a little experience soon teaches her she " did
not very well then know what a desert was."
Scotch mists and mountain blasts dispel the fancy
picture, and, after a brief period of acute wretched-
ness, the really heartless victim of a so-called love
match becomes the zealous promoter of mercenary
connections.

Miss Ferrier then introduces us to the next generation, where any attempt at dogmatism about love
becomes hazardous.

" Love is a passion that has been much talked of,
often described, and little understood. Cupid has
many counterfeits going about the world, who pass
very well with those whose minds are capable of passion,
but not of love.   These Birmingham Cupids have many
votaries among boarding-school misses, militia officers,
and milliners' apprentices, who marry upon the mutual
faith of blue eyes and scarlet coats ; have dirty houses

and squalling children, and hate each other most
delectably. Then there is another species for more
refined souls, which owes its birth to the works of
Rousseau, Goethe, Cottin, etc. Its success depends
very much upon rocks, woods, and waterfalls ; and it
generally ends in daggers, pistols, poisons, or Doctors'
Commons."

It would seem that even the heroine is, like
Emily in *Udolpho*, rather at sea concerning the
proper distinction between virtue and taste.

She is " religious—what mind of any excellence is
not ? but hers is the religion of poetry, of taste, of
feeling, of impulse, of any and everything but Chris-
tianity." The worthy youth who loved her " saw
much of fine natural feeling, but in vain sought for any
guiding principle of duty. Her mind seemed as a lovely,
flowery, pathless waste, whose sweets exhaled in vain ;
all was graceful luxuriance, but all was transient and
perishable in its loveliness. No plant of immortal
growth grew there, no ' flowers worthy of Paradise.' "

Inevitably the dear creature is captivated, at
first sight, by any good-looking villain : " There
might, perhaps, be something of *hauteur* in his lofty
bearing ; but it was so qua...fied by the sportive
gaiety of his manners, that it seemed nothing more
than that elegant and graceful sense of his own
superiority, to which, even without arrogance, he
could not be insensible."

The hero will no doubt require time before he can
·stand up against so fine a gentleman ; but justice
requires his ultimate triumph, since, in Miss Ferrier's
judgment, a " good moral " was always essential to
fiction.

" I don't think, like all penny-book manufacturers,
that 'tis absolutely necessary that the good boys and
girls should be rewarded,and the naughty ones punished.
Yet, I think, where there is much tribulation, 'tis fitter
it should be the *consequence*, rather than the *cause*,
of misconduct or frailty.   You'll say that rule is absurd,
inasmuch as it is not observed in human life.   That I
allow ; but we know the inflictions of Providence are
for wise purposes, therefore our reason willingly sub-
mits to them.   But, as the only good purpose of a book
is to inculcate morality, and convey some lesson of
instruction as well as delight, I do not see that what is
called a *good moral* can be dispensed with in a work of
fiction."

Miss Ferrier, in fact, would have no hand in the
" raw head and bloody bone schemes " in which
Miss Clavering (who wrote " The History of Mrs.
Douglas " in *Marriage*) had, apparently, invited
her to collaborate, and chose rather to exemplify
her own theories in three very similar stories :
Marriage (1818), *The Inheritance* (1824), and *Destiny*
(1831). Urged, again and again, to supplement

these successes, she made " two attempts to write
something else, but could not please herself, and
would not publish *anything* "—a most praiseworthy
resolution.

She has left us an entertaining account of
her " plan " for *Marriage*, which may well serve for
an exact description of her actual achievement.

" I do not recollect ever to have seen the sudden
transition of a high-bred English beauty, who thinks
she can sacrifice all for love, to an uncomfortable,
solitary, Highland dwelling, among tall, red-haired
sisters and grim-faced aunts. Don't you think this
would make a good opening of the piece ? Suppose
each of us [1] try our hands on it ; the moral to be deduced
from that is to warn all young ladies against runaway
matches, and the character and fate of the two sisters
would be *unexceptionable*. I expect it will be the
first book every wise matron will put into the hand of
her daughter, and even the reviewers will relax of their
severity in favour of the morality of this little work.
Enchanting sight ! already do I behold myself arrayed
in an old mouldy covering, thumbed and creased and
filled with dog's ears. I hear the enchanting sound
of some sentimental miss, the shrill pipe of some anti-
quated spinster, or the hoarse grumbling of some
incensed dowager as they severally enquire for me at
the circulating library, and are assured by the master
that it is in such demand that, though he has thirteen

---

[1] She is writing, again, to Miss Clavering.

copies, they are insufficient to answer the calls upon it ; but that each one of them may depend upon having the very first that comes in ! ! ! "

The interest, in these novels, is not awakened by any subtle characterisation or by serious sympathy with the dramatis personæ. It depends rather upon caustic wit, accurate local colour, a picture of manners, and a "museum of abnormalities."

Miss Ferrier's nice distinctions between the "well-bred," and her photographs of vulgarity, may claim to rival Miss Burney's.

"Mrs. St. Clair, for example, was considerably annoyed by the manners of Lady Charles, which made her feel her own as something unwieldy and overgrown ; like a long train, they were both out of the way and in the way, and she did not know very well how to dispose of them. Indeed, few things can be more irritating than for those who have hitherto piqued themselves upon the abundance of their manner, to find all at once that they have a great deal too much, and that no one is inclined to take it off their hands, and that, in short, it is dead stock."

Mrs. Bluemit's tea-party, again, reveals the Blue-Stockings in all their glory ; while Mr. Augustus Larkins—with his " regular features, very pink eyes, very black eyebrows, and what was intended for a very smart expression "—forcibly recalls Mr. Smith of Snow Hill. His ideal of dress and manners was evidently shared by Bob and Davy Black, who were

" dressed in all the extremes of the reigning fashions —small waists, brush-heads, stiff collars, iron heels, and switches. Like many other youths they were distinctly of opinion that ' dress makes the man.' . . . Perhaps, after all, that is a species of humility rather to be admired in those who, feeling themselves destitute of mental qualifications, trust to the abilities of their tailor and hairdresser for gaining them the goodwill of the world."

It must be admitted that Miss Ferrier's obviously spontaneous delight in satire has occasionally tempted her beyond the limits of artistic realism. Her miniature of the M'Dow, for example, has all the objectionable qualities which revive our prefer- ence for the " elegancies " of romance.

" Here Miss M'Dow was disencumbered of her pelisse and bonnet, and exhibited a coarse, blubber-lipped, sun-burnt visage, with staring sea-green eyes, a quantity of rough sandy hair, and mulatto neck, with merely a rim of white round her shoulders. . . . The gloves were then taken off, and a pair of thick mulberry paws set at liberty."

No such criticism, however applies to those full-length portraits of the inimitable Aunts in *Marrriage*—the " sensible " Miss Jacky, Miss Nicky, who was " not wanting for sense either," and Miss Grizzy, the great letter-writer. " Their life was one continued *fash* about everything or nothing " ; and if a " sensible woman " generally means " a very disagreeable, obstinate, illiberal director of all men, women, and children," the Aunts were really " well-meaning, kind-hearted, and, upon the whole, good-tempered " old ladies, whose garrulous absurdities are a perpetual delight.

Again, Miss Pratt (of *The Inheritance*) has certain obvious affinities to the inimitable Miss Bates ; as Mr. M'Dow (in *Destiny*) recalls Collins ; and the creation of that good soul, Molly Macaulay, bears solitary evidence to Miss Ferrier's seldom-exerted powers of sympathetic subtlety.

We are tempted to wonder if there be any particular significance in the fact that, though Miss Ferrier wrote *Marriage* almost immediately after the appearance of *Sense and Sensibility*, she did not publish it till seven years later.[1]   If, during that interval, she felt compelled to study the supreme

---

[1] When *Pride and Prejudice, Emma,* and *Mansfield Park* had all been published.

excellences of a sister-authoress, it is clear that she wisely abandoned any attempt at imitation.   Her work, as we have seen, directly follows Miss Burney's, and should be properly regarded in relation to *Evelina* and *Cecilia* ; reflecting Society—and the upstart—of a slightly later generation, then flourishing in North Britain.

MARY RUSSELL MITFORD (1787–1855) is the only writer on record who has deliberately declared herself a disciple.

" Of course, I shall copy as closely as I can nature and Miss Austen—keeping, like her, to genteel country life ; or rather going a little lower, perhaps ; and, I am afraid, with more of sentiment and less of humour.   I do not *intend* to commit these deliquencies, mind.   I *mean* to keep as playful as I can ; but I am afraid they will happen in spite of me. . . . It will be called—at least, I mean it so to be—*Our Village*; will consist of essays, and characters, and stories, chiefly of country life, in the manner of the *Sketch Book,* connected by unity of locality and purpose.   It is exceedingly playful and lively, and I think you will like it.   Charles Lamb (the matchless *Elia* of the London Magazine) says nothing so fresh and characteristic has appeared for a long time."

It *was* called *Our Village* ; and appeared in parts between 1824 and 1832, the earlier series being the

best, because afterwards she wrote for remuneration
—when " I would rather scrub floors, if I could get
as much by that healthier, more respectable, and
more feminine employment,"—a declaration which
prepares us for the criticism that, though in her
own day she was accused of copying the " literal "
manner of Crabbe and Teniers, she was at heart a
frank sentimentalist. " Are your characters and
descriptions true ? " asked her friend Sir William
Elford ; and she replied, " Yes ! yes ! yes ! as true
as is well possible. You, as a great landscape
painter, know that, in painting a favourite scene,
you do a little embellish, and can't help it, you
avail yourself of happy accidents of atmosphere,
and *if anything be ugly, you strike it out*, or if anything be wanting, you put it in. But still the
picture is a likeness."

Assuredly Miss Mitford was no realist, nor was
her imitation servile. Once she expressed a desire
that Miss Austen had shown " a little more taste,
a little more perception of the graceful " ; and, in
such matters, as in culture, she was herself far more
professional. But although she could describe, and
even " compose," with a charm of her own which
almost defies analysis, Miss Mitford's powers were

strictly limited. The " country-town " atmosphere
of *Belford Regis* lacks spontaneity ; and *Atherton*,
her only attempt at a novel, is wanting in varied
incident or motion   Readers attracted by mere
simplicity, however, will feel always a peculiar
affection for Miss Mitford, that would be increased
by her " Letters " which she describes as " just
like so many bottles of ginger-beer, bouncing and
frothy, and flying in everybody's face."

Christopher North remarked in *Noctes Am-
brosianæ* that her writings were " pervaded by a
genuine rural spirit—the spirit of Merry England.
Every line bespeaks the lady."

And the " Shepherd " replied :

" I admire Miss Mitford just excessively. I dinna
wunner at her being able to write sae weel as she does
about drawing-rooms wi' sofas and settees, and about
the fine folk in them seeing themsels in lookin-glasses
frae tap to tae ; but what puzzles the like o' me, is
her pictures o' poachers, and tinklers, and pottery-
trampers, and ither neerdoweels, and o' huts and hovels
without riggin' by the wayside, and the cottages o'
honest puir men, and byres, and barns, and stackyards,
and merry-makins at winter ingles, and courtship
aneath trees, and at the gable-end of farm houses,
'tween lads and lasses as laigh in life as the servants
in her father's ha'. That's the puzzle, and that's the

praise. But ae word explains a'—Genius—Genius,
wull a' the metafhizzians in the warld ever expound
that mysterious monosyllable.—Nov. 1826.''

MARY WOLLSTONECRAFT SHELLEY (1797–1851)
has no place in the development of women's work
in fiction, since her one novel, *Frankenstein*, belongs
to no type that has been attempted before or
since, though it is often roughly described as a
throw-back to the School of Terror. The conception of a man-made Monster, with human feelings—
of pathetic loneliness and brutal cruelty—was
eminently characteristic of an age which hankered
after the byways of Science, imagined unlimited
possibilities from the extension of knowledge,
and was never tired of speculation. Inevitably the
daughter of William Godwin had some didactic
intentions ; and her " Preface " declares her " by
no means indifferent to the manner in which whatever moral tendencies exist in the sentiments or
characters it contains shall affect the reader ; yet
my chief concern in this respect has been limited
to the avoiding of the enervating effects of the
novels of the present day, and to the exhibition of
the amiableness of domestic affection and the excellence of universal virtue." Among other things,

Mrs. Shelley betrays her sympathy with Rousseau's
ideal of the " Man Natural," and with vegetarian-
ism.   In a mood of comparative reasonableness and
humanity the Monster promises, under certain
conditions, to abandon his revenge and bury
himself in the " Wilds of South America."

" My food is not that of man ; I do not destroy the
lamb and the kid, to glut my appetite ; acorns and
berries will afford me sufficient nourishment. My
companion will be of the same nature as myself, and
will be content with the same fare. We shall make
our bed of dried leaves ; the sun will shine on us as
on man, and will ripen our food."

The ethical struggle, with which Mrs. Shelley
has here concerned herself, arises from circumstances beyond the pale of experience ; but her
solution is characteristic, and echoes the spirit
of Shelley himself. Frankenstein, " in a fit of enthusiastic madness, has created a rational creature,"
who, finding himself hated by mankind, resolves
to punish his creator. He promises, however,
to abstain from murdering Frankenstein's family,
if that man of science will make for him a female
companion with whom he may peacefully retire to
the wilderness. Obviously the temptation is great.
Frankenstein's brother has been already destroyed :

it would seem his duty to protect his father and his
wife.   But, on the other hand,

" My duties towards my fellow-creatures had greater
claims to my attention, *because they included a greater
proportion of happiness or misery*.   Urged by this view,
I refused, and I did right in refusing, to create a companion for the first creature."

There is no professional art in the story of
Frankenstein, though it has a certain gloomy and
perverse power.   It is told in letters from an arctic
explorer " To Mrs. Saville, England " ; and the
monster's own life-story, with the only revelation
of his emotions, is narrated within this narrative,
in a monologue to Frankenstein.

It is uncertain whether the work would ever
have been remembered, or revived, apart from our
natural interest in the author ; although, so far
as it has any similarity with other work, it belongs
to a class of novels which English writers have
seldom attempted, and never accomplished with
any distinction.

FRANCES TROLLOPE (1780–1863) has been so
completely overshadowed by her son Anthony—
himself a distinguished practitioner in the domestic

novel—that few readers to-day are aware that her fertile pen produced a " whole army of novels and books of travel, sometimes pouring into the libraries at the rate of nine volumes a year." She began her career—curiously enough, when she was past fifty—by a severely satirical attack on the United States, entitled *Domestic Manners of the Americans* ; and her first novel, *The Abbess*, did not appear till 1833. She was essentially feminine in the enthusiasm of her tirades against various practices in her generation, and has been freely criticised for want of taste. *The Vicar of Wrex-hill* (1837), indeed, is coloured by a violent prejudice which goes far to justify this objection, and may even excuse the disparaging deduction on women's intellect drawn by a contemporary reviewer, who thus characterises her spirited defence of " oppressed Orthodoxy " :

" It is a great pity that the heroine ever set forth on such a foolish errand ; she has only harmed herself and her cause (as a bad advocate always will) and had much better have remained at home pudding-making or stocking-mending, than have meddled with what she understands so ill.

" In the first place (we speak it with due respect for the sex) she is guilty of a fault which is somewhat tco common among them ; and having very little, except prejudice, on which to found an opinion, she makes up for want of argument by a wonderful fluency of abuse. A *woman's religion is chiefly that of the heart, and not of the head.* She goes through, for the most part, no dreadful stages of doubt, no changes of faith : *she loves God as she loves her husband by a kind of instinctive devotion.* Faith is a passion with her, not a calculation ; so that, in the faculty of believing, though they far exceed the other sex, in the power of convincing they fall far short of them." [1]

More than one woman writer has risen, of later years, triumphantly to confute any such complacent masculine superiority ; but it must be admitted that Mrs. Trollope is scarcely judicial in the venom she pours out so eloquently upon the head of her " Vicar," his worshippers, and his accomplices. This was not quite the direction in which women could most wisely develop the domestic novel in her day ; while they still—like the Brontës, but in a spirit quite alien to Jane Austen's—upheld " that manly passion for superiority which leads *our masters* to covet in a companion chosen for life . . . that species of weakness which is often said to be the most attractive feature in the female character." It is, again, a curious

[1] *Fraser's Magazine,* Jan. 1838.

want of taste which allows her to dwell upon the pleasure experienced by a comparatively respectable young man in making a little girl of eight tipsy—though he is the Vicar's son.

But, on the other hand, there is considerable power and much sprightly humour in the story. Mrs. Trollope's *good* (*i.e.* orthodox) people are really delightful, and admirably characterised. The *genuine* piety of Rosalind, the Irish heiress, is most artistically united to graceful vivacity and natural charm : the testy Sir Gilbert is perfectly matched with Lady Harrington : and the three young Mowbrays are drawn from life. The study of Henrietta Cartwright, driven to atheism by the hypocrisy of her horrible father, has all the force of a real human tragedy ; and, if the villainy of Evangelicism is exaggerated, it is painted with graphic humour. She works from nature, and finds excellent " copy " in the parish.

Mrs. Trollope, in fact, has left us proof in abundance that women had learnt to " write with ease " ; if, in her case over-production and misplaced zeal have led to an abuse of her talents.

HARRIET MARTINEAU (1802–1876), " Queen of

philanthropists," has left a stamp of almost passionate sincerity on everything she wrote. From
earliest days she declared that her " chief subordinate object in life was the cultivation of her
intellectual powers, with a view to the instruction
of others by her writings." Believing herself the
servant of humanity, she sought to save souls by
the diffusion of a little knowledge.

Inevitably, under such influence, her work was
always didactic ; whether inspired by the orthodox
faith of her earlier years or the Atkinson-
interpretation of Comte she afterwards espoused :
whether directed towards social reform, or expressed
in narrative and biography. The greater number
of her publications, whether or no actually written
for the press, contain those qualities which make
the best journalism ; and, though occasionally
capricious and " superior " in private judgment,
her brief critical biographies, from the *Daily News*,
are masterpieces in the vignette. She knew
" everybody " in her day ; and contributed much
to the thirst for " information," reasonably applied,
which characterised our grandfathers.

But, as a novelist. she has two special claims
to notice. Her " Playfellow Series " (embracing

Feats on the Fiord, The Crofton Boys, and *The Peasant and the Prince*) are living to-day among the few priceless inherited treasures of literature. Less obviously didactic than the Edgeworth "nursery classics," they have certain similar characteristics of spontaneity, sympathetic understanding, and simple directness. Each occupied with quite different subjects, they are informed by the same spirit, excite the same kind of pleasure, and—for all their decided, but *not* obtrusive, moralising—appeal to the same healthy taste. By those to whom their life-like young people have been among the chosen friends of childhood, the memories will never fade.

Miss Martineau's adult narratives have less distinction; although her *Hour and the Man* is a creditable effort in the historic form, and *Deerbrook* has much emotional power. To our taste the tone of the latter must be criticised for its somewhat sensational religiosity, and for the priggish perfection of its "white" characters. But, on the other hand, there is subtlety in contrasts among the "undesirables"; genuine pathos in, for example, the description of Mrs. Enderby's death; and plenty of artistic "interest" in the plot: nor can we neglect mention of the remarkable portrait of Morris, the servant and most real friend to her " young ladies."

We cannot avoid, in conclusion, some reference to a distinction elaborated in an early chapter between the drudgery of " *teaching* " and the " sublime delights of *education* " : wherein the author quaintly remarks that a visiting governess can " do little more than stand between children and the faults of the people about them " ; betraying herein the normal prejudice of the pedagogue against the parent.

Similar theories clearly inspire the eloquence— of a later chapter—upon a thorny subject on which the author achieved some pioneer work in her own life.

" ' Cannot you tell me,' enquires the persecuted heroine, ' of some way in which a woman may earn money ? '

" ' A woman ? ' is the stern reply. ' What rate of woman ? Do you mean yourself ? That question is easily answered. A woman from the uneducated classes can get a subsistence by washing and cooking, by milking cows and going into service, and, in some parts of the kingdom, by working in a cotton mill, or burnishing plate, as you have no doubt seen for yourself at Birmingham. But, for an educated woman, a woman

with the powers God gave her religiously improved,
with a reason which lays life open before her, an understanding which surveys science as its appropriate
task, and a conscience which would make every species
of responsibility safe,—for such a woman there is in all
England no chance of subsistence but teaching—that
sort of ineffectual teaching, which can never counter-
vail the education of circumstances—and for which
not one in a thousand is fit,—or by being a superior
Miss Nares—the feminine gender of the tailor and
hatter.' "

MRS. GASKELL (1810–1865) must always be remembered as authoress of *Cranford*, which has
startling similarities to the work of Jane Austen,
and excels her in pathos. If Fanny Burney immortalised "sensibility," and Jane Austen created
"the lady," Mrs. Gaskell may well be called " The
Apologist of Gentility." She taught us that it was
possible to be genteel without being vulgar ; and
her "refined females," if enslaved to elegance and
propriety, are ladies in the best sense of the word.

"Although they know all each other's proceedings, they are exceedingly indifferent to each
other's opinions." They are " very independent of
fashion ; as they observe : ' What does it signify
how we dress here at Cranford, where everybody
knows us ? ' and if they go from home, their reason

is equally cogent : ' What does it signify how we dress here, where nobody knows us ? ' '' We may smile at their ingenious devices for concealing poverty, their grotesque small conventions, their horror at any allusions to death or other causes for genuine emotion, and their love of gossip ; but our superiority stands rebuked before simple Miss Matty's sense of honour " as a shareholder," and before the " meeting of the Cranford ladies " for the generous contribution of their " mites in a secret and concealed manner." As Miss Pole expresses it, " We are none of us what may be called rich, though we all possess a genteel competency, sufficient for tastes that are elegant and refined, and would not, if they could, be vulgarly ostentatious " ; and they fully appreciated the true charity of " showing consideration for the feelings of delicate independence existing in the mind of every refined female."

Here, indeed, as in almost every thought or deed of their uneventful existence, our grandmothers can teach us that the eager interest in our neighbours, which we are accustomed to brand as vulgar and impertinent, was in actual fact a powerful incentive to Christian practices. There is a passage in *Cranford* which would baffle the most elaborate statistics of ordered philanthropy, as it must silence the protest of false pride, and remain an invulnerable argument against the isolation of modern life. " I had often occasion to notice," observes the visitor, " the use that was made of fragments and small opportunities in Cranford : the rose-leaves that were gathered ere they fell, to make a *pot-pourri* for some one who had no garden ; the little bundles of lavender-flowers sent to strew the drawers of some town-dweller, or to burn in the bedroom of some invalid. Things that many would despise, and actions which it seemed scarcely worth while to perform, were all attended to in Cranford."

Nor were Miss Matilda Jenkyns and her friends deficient in any outward show of true breeding. Despite the most astonishing vagaries of taste in dress, language, and behaviour, they were dignified by instinct, and, on all occasions of moment, revealed a natural manner that is above reproach. Their simple-minded innocence and genuine humility never tempted them to pass over impertinence or tolerate vulgarity, and their powers of delicate reproof were unrivalled. We cannot

admire the " green turban " of Miss Matty's dream,
or share her dread of the frogs in Paris not agreeing
with Mr. Holbrook ; we should have been ashamed,
maybe, to assist her in " chasing the sunbeams "
over her new carpet ; and we may detect sour
grapes in Miss Pole's outcry against that " kind of
attraction which she, for one, would be ashamed
to have " ; yet I fancy the best of us would covet
admission to Cranford society, and be proud to
number its leaders among our dearest friends.

In fact, the artistic achievement of *Cranford* is
the creation of an atmosphere. Like the authors
of *Evelina* and *of Emma*, Mrs. Gaskell is frankly
feminine, and not superior to the smallest detail
of parochial gossip ; but while the ideals of refinement portrayed are more akin to Miss Burney's
(allowing for altered social conditions), her methods
of portraiture more nearly resemble Miss Austen's.
She depends, even less, upon excitement, mystery,
or crime, and *Cranford*, indeed, may be described
as " a novel without a hero," without a plot, and
without a love-scene. Miss Brown's death is the
one *event* with which we are brought, as it were,
face to face throughout the whole sixteen chapters.
The realities of life, whether sad or joyful, are

enacted behind the scenes and never used for dramatic effect, a reticence most striking in the incident of Captain Brown's heroic death. They serve only to reveal the strong and true hearts of those whose dainty old-world mannerisms have already secured our sympathy.

Mrs. Gaskell has *left out* even more than Jane Austen of the ordinary materials of fiction (though she is an adept at pathos), and her characters are equally living. She has less wit, but almost as much humour.

The most obvious limitation of *Cranford*, indeed, is more apparent than real. As everyone will remember, " all the holders of houses " are women. " If a married couple settles in the town, somehow the gentleman disappears ; he is either fairly frightened to death by being the only man in the Cranford evening tea-parties, or he is accounted for by being at his regiment, his ship, or closely engaged in business all the week in the great neighbouring commercial town of Drumble, distant only twenty miles on a railroad. In short, whatever does become of the gentlemen, they are not at Cranford. What could they do there ? . . . A man is *so* in the way in the house."

Even the Rector dare not attend a public entertainment unless " guarded by troops of his own sex—the National School boys whom he had treated to the performance." The " neat maid-servants " were never allowed " followers " ; and it was Miss Matty's chief consolation in starting her little business that " she did not think men ever bought tea." She was afraid of men. " They had such sharp, loud ways with them, and did up accounts, and counted their change so quickly."

Yet, in fact, the masculine element in *Cranford* comes frequently to the front ; and the men's characters are drawn with no less firmness of outline than the women's. Miss Matty derives much from her Reverend father — deceased, from that sturdy yeoman Thomas Holbrook, and from " Mr. Peter." It is Captain Brown, and no other, whose misfortunes unmask the real tenderness of Miss Jenkyns herself ; and the good Mr. Hoggins occasions the only serious discord narrated in the select circle of " elegant females," to whom his uncouth surname was a perpetual affront. The unfortunate conjurer, Signor Brunoni, otherwise Mr. Brown (was it accident or design, we wonder, which gave him

the same plebeian name as the gallant Captain ?) ;
his brother Thomas ;   the great Mr. Mulliner,
" who seemed never to have forgotten his condescension in coming to live at Cranford " ; honest
farmer Dobson ; and dear, blundering Jim Hearn,
whose tactful notion of kindness was " to keep
out of your way as much as he could " ;   each
played their part in the lives of their lady-betters.

Thomas Holbrook, his quotations from Shakespeare, George Herbert, and Tennyson ; his love
of Nature ;   his two-pronged forks ;   and his
charming " counting-house," have no less subtle
originality than any character in the whole
book ; and we should hesitate to name any record
of perfect fidelity, without sentimentalism, to be
compared with the simply chivalrous and cheerful
attentions of this gentleman of seventy to the old
lady who had refused, at the bidding of father and
sister, " to marry below her rank."   One can
only echo the pious aspiration (so touching in its
unselfish abandonment of a cherished ideal), by
which alone Miss Matty betrayed the emotions
excited by the visit to her old lover : " ' God
forbid,' said she, in a low voice, ' that I should
grieve any young hearts.' "

Holbrook, moreover, had been no doubt largely responsible for encouraging the inherent good qualities of Miss Matty's scapegrace brother (afterwards the popular Mr. Peter), whose thoughtless pranks form so strange, and yet so fitting, a background to those finished miniature-sketches of the stern Rector and his sweet young wife. It is, indeed, a fine instance of poetical justice by which Mr. Peter is allowed, in his old age, to bestow a richly merited peace and comfort, in addition to the diversion of masculine society, upon the very sister whose early life had been so terribly clouded by his misdeeds.

One is almost tempted to say that Mrs. Gaskell does scant justice to the first invader of the Amazons, when she refers to Captain Brown as "a tame man about the house." Yet those of us with sufficient imagination to realise the firm exclusiveness of Miss Deborah Jenkyns, should appreciate the significance of the phrase. The military gentleman, "who was not ashamed to be poor," only found his way to that lady's good graces by sterling qualities of true manliness. He was "even admitted in the tabooed hours before twelve," because no errand of kindness was beneath his dignity or beyond his patience.

Miss Matty expresses the prevailing sentiment about men, as she has done on most subjects worthy of attention, with that " love of peace and kindliness," which " makes all of us better when we are near her."

" I don't mean to deny that men are troublesome in a house. I don't judge from my own experience, for my father was neatness itself, and wiped his shoes in coming in as carefully as any woman ; but still a man has a sort of knowledge of what should be done in difficulties, that it is very pleasant to have one at hand ready to lean upon. Now Lady Glenmire " (whose engagement to Mr. Hoggins was the occasion of this gentle homily), " instead of being tossed about and wondering where she is to settle, will be certain of a home among pleasant and kind people, such as our good Miss Pole and Mrs. Forrester. And Mr. Hoggins is really a very personable man ; and so far as his manners—why, if they are not very polished, I have known people with very good hearts, and very clever minds too, who were not what some people reckoned refined, but who were tender and true." Again : " Don't be frightened by Miss Pole from being married. I can fancy it may be a very happy state, and a little credulity helps one through life very smoothly—better than always doubting and doubting, and seeing difficulties and disagreeables in every-thing."

The finality of the above quotations may further remind us of an unexpected conclusion to which a careful study of *Cranford* must compel the critic. Despite its apparent inconsequence, the desultory nature of the narrative, and its surprising inno-cence of plot, the work is composed with an almost perfect sense of dramatic unity. In reality every event, however trivial or serious, every shade of character, however subtle or obvious, is at once subordinate and essential to the character of the heroine. A heroine, " not far short of sixty, whose looks were against her," may not attract the habitual novel-reader ; but unless we submit to the charm of Miss Matty's personality, we have misread *Cranford*. Deborah, the domineering, had not so much real strength of character, and serves only as a foil to her sister's wider sympathies ; the superficial quickness of Miss Pole never ulti-mately misled her friend's finer judgment ; the (temporary) snobbishness of the Honourable Mrs. Jamieson troubles her heart indeed, but leaves her dignity unruffled ; and the other members of the circle scarcely aspire to be more than humble admirers of the " Rector's daughter." Miss Matty, of course, is sublimely unconscious of her own influence, and the authoress very nearly deceives us into fancying her equally innocent. But she gives away the secret in her farewell sentence; and I, for one, would not quarrel with her for pointing the moral. Miss Matty can never lose her place in the Gallery of the Immortals, and we would not neglect to honour the painter's name.

Mrs. Gaskell, in *Cranford*, may claim to have reached perfection by one finished achievement; which embodies the ideal to which we conceive that the work in fiction peculiar to women had been, more or less consciously, directed from the beginning. Probably the art would have been less flawless, if applied—as it was by sister-novelists—to a wider range of persons and subjects. Nothing of quite this kind has been again attempted, and it is not likely that such an attempt would succeed.

We should only notice, in passing, that Mrs. Gaskell left other admirable, and quite feminine, work on more ordinary lines. *Wives and Daughters* is a delightful love story; while *North and South* and *Mary Barton* are almost the first examples of that keen interest in social problems, and the life of the poor, in legitimate novels (not fiction-tracts), which we shall find so favourite a topic of women from her generation until to-day.

A LONELY SOUL

(Charlotte Brontë, 1816–1855)

The genius of Charlotte Brontë presents several characteristics which do not belong to the more or less orderly development of the earlier women's work. In the first place she is primarily a romancist, depending far more on emotional analysis than on the exact portraiture of everyday life. Though her materials, like theirs, are gained entirely from personal experience, she clothes them with a passionate imagination very foreign to anything in Miss Burney or Jane Austen. She writes, in other words, because her emotions are forced into speech by that very intensity; not at all from amused observation of life. It would be difficult, indeed, to find outside her few remarkable stories so powerful an expression of passion as felt by women—who do not, as a rule, admit the power of such stormy emotions. Her work is further remarkable for being mainly inspired by memory; while the recognition of responsiveness in women leads her to paint *mutual* passion as it has been seldom revealed elsewhere.

Much has been written of late years concerning the life of Charlotte Brontë, and we have been told that the mystery is solved at last. For despite the almost startling frankness of Mrs. Gaskell's famous *Life*; despite the intimate character of many of her published letters ; it has always been recognised that the Charlotte Brontë of the biographers was *not* the Charlotte Brontë of *Jane Eyre* and *Villette*. Now that we have the letters to Monsieur Heger, however, it seems to be a prevailing conclusion that reconciliation, and understanding, are possible. If Charlotte Brontë, like her own Lucy Snowe, was in love with " her master " ; if he was perfectly happy in his married life and, however responsive to enthusiastic admiration, found warmer feelings both embarrassing and vexatious ; we have discovered the tragedy which fired her imagination, the utter loneliness which taught her to dwell so bitterly on the aching void of unreturned affection, to idealise so romantically the rapture of marriage. Personally we are disposed to accept these interpretations, but not to rely on them for everything. To begin

with, it is always dangerous to dwell upon any
" explanation " of genius ; and, in the second place,
it was not Charlotte Brontë's experiences (which
others have suffered), but the nature awakened
by them, which determined their artistic expression.

Part of the difficulty arises from the two almost
contradictory methods in which she " worked
up " her stories. She had remarkable powers of
observation and borrowed from real life as reck-
lessly as Shakespeare borrowed plots, with very
similar indifference to possible criticism. In this
matter, indeed, she cannot be altogether acquitted
of malice or spite ; and we do not learn with un-
mixed pleasure how many " originals " actually
existed for her dramatis personæ.

But, on the other hand, if " every person and
a large proportion of the incidents were copied
from life," the emotional power of her work is
entirely imaginative. As pictures of life, her
stories are inadequate and unsatisfying, partly
because there is so much in human nature and in
life which does not interest her : so much of which
she knew nothing ; and she is only at home in
the heart of her subject. Here again she is in no
way realistic—as was Jane Austen in manners or

George Eliot in emotion—but entirely romantic,
however original her conception of romance. Her
heroes and heroines are as far from everyday
humanity, and as ideal and visionary, as Mrs.
Radcliffe's, though she does not, of course, follow
the " rules " of romance : rather creating out of
her own brain a new heaven and a new earth,
inhabited by a people that know not God or man.

Apart from the rude awakening at Brussels,
again, she exhibited in private correspondence
by turns the strange contrasts between common
sense and emotionalism which mark her work.

She defines the " right path " as " that which
necessitates the greatest sacrifice of self-interest " :
she thinks, " if you can respect a person before
marriage, moderate love at least will come after ;
and as to intense passion, I am convinced that that
is no desirable feeling."

She advises her best friend that

" no young lady should fall in love till the offer has
been made, accepted, the marriage ceremony per-
formed, and the first half-year of wedded life has passed
away. A woman may then begin to love, but with
great precaution, very coolly, very moderately, very
rationally. If she ever loves so much that a harsh word
or a cold look cuts her to the heart, she is a fool.

If she ever loves so much that her husband's will is her
law, and that she has got into the habit of watching
his looks in order that she may anticipate his wishes,
she will soon be a neglected fool."

On the other hand, " if you knew my thoughts,
the dreams that absorb me, and the fiery imagination that at times eats me up, and makes me feel
society, as it is, insipid, you would pity me and
I daresay despise me."

Her emotion on first seeing the sea is absolutely
overpowering ; and surely we know the woman
who insisted on visiting a maidservant " attacked
by a violent fever," fearlessly entered her room
in spite of every remonstrance, " threw herself
on the bed beside her, and repeatedly kissed her
burning brow."

Experience with her, in fact, had never been
confined to the external happenings, which can
be accumulated, with more or less sympathy,
by the biographer ; and her own declaration of
how she worked up episodes outside her own experience may be applied, without much modifica-
tion, to her manipulation of that experience itself.
Asked whether the description of taking opium
in *Villette* was based on knowledge,

" She replied that she had never, to her knowledge, taken a grain of it in any shape, but that she had followed the process she always adopted when she had to describe anything which had not fallen within her own experience ; she had thought intently on it for many and many a night before falling to sleep—wondering what it was like or how it would be—till at length, sometimes after the progress of her story had been arrested at this one point for weeks, she wakened up in the morning with all clear before her, as if she had in reality gone through the experience, and then could describe it word for word as it had happened."

It is obvious that, if no less feminine than her predecessors, the nature and methods of Charlotte Brontë would produce very different work from theirs. In narrative and description she remains domestic and middle-class. She does not adopt the " high " notions of aristocracy, she does not plunge into the mysteries of crime. Her plots are laid " at home," so to speak, and among the professional classes or small gentry with whom she was personally familiar. The only material which may be noticed as a new departure is derived from her particular experiences in schools in England and abroad, combined with her intimate knowledge of the governess and the tutor. In *Shirley*, again, she is one of the earliest women to devote any serious attention to the progress of trade and the introduction of machinery, with its effect on the social problems of the working classes.

In construction, on the other hand, she is admittedly inferior to her predecessors, since her plots are melodramatic, and her characterisation is disturbed by a somewhat morbid analysis of unusual passion. Her feminine ideal has no parallel in the " sensibility " of Fanny Burney or the sprightly " calm " of Jane Austen. Its most distinguishing characteristic is, naturally, revealed in the attitude assumed towards man. The hero, the ideal lover, is always " the Master " of the heroine. Jane Eyre being a governess and Lucy Snowe a pupil, we might perhaps miss the full significance of the phrase ; but even the strong-minded Shirley refuses Sir Philip Nunnely, because, among other reasons, " he is very amiable—very excellent— truly estimable, but *not my master* ; not in one point. I could not trust myself with his happiness : I would not undertake the keeping of it for thousands ; I will accept no hand that cannot hold me in check."

Jane Austen once playfully accused herself of having dared to draw a heroine who had fallen in

love without first having ascertained the gentleman's feeling. This is the normal achievement—
in Charlotte Brontë—not only of heroines, but *of
all women*. It is, of course, almost inevitable that
since, in her work (as in those of her sister-authors)
we see everything *through the minds* of the women
characters, we should learn the state of their heart
first; but, in most cases at least, it is certain that
we are in as much doubt as the heroine herself
concerning the man's feelings, and it is fairly
obvious that often he has actually not made up
his mind. The women in Charlotte Brontë, in
fact, are what we now call "doormats." They
delight in *serving* the Beloved; they expect him to
be a superior being, with more control over his
emotions; less dependent on emotion or even on
domestic comfort, appropriately concerned with
matters not suited to feminine intellects, and
accustomed to "keep his own counsel" about the
important decisions of life.

It is her achievement to have secured our enthusiastic devotion to "females" so thoroughly
Early Victorian; for the heroines of Charlotte
Brontë remain some of the most striking figures
in fiction. They are really heroic, and, while glory-

ing in their self-imposed limitations, become vital
by their intensity and depth.   Jane Austen once
quietly demonstrated the natural "constancy"
of women ; Charlotte Brontë paints this virtue in
fiery colours across all her work.   Her incidental,
but most marked, preference for *plain* heroines—
inspired, apparently, by passionate jealousy of
popular beauty—serves to emphasise the abnormal
capacity for passion and fidelity which, in her
judgment, the power of easily exciting general admiration apparently tends to diminish.

A contemporary reviewer in the *Quarterly*—
probably Lockhart — found this type of women
disgustingly sly.   The whole of *Jane Eyre*, indeed,
fills him with holy horror, which is genuine enough,
though expressed with most ungentlemanly virulence, and prefaced with the extraordinary suggestion that " Jane Eyre is *merely another Pamela* (!)
. . . a small, plain, odd creature, who has been
brought up dry upon school learning, and somewhat stunted accordingly in mind and body, and
who is thrown upon the world as ignorant of its
ways, and as destitute of its friendships, as a ship-
wrecked mariner upon a strange coast."   Rochester,
on the other hand, he finds " captious and Turklike

... a strange brute, somewhat in the Squire Western style of absolute and capricious eccentricity." The book is guilty of the " highest moral offence a novel-writer can commit, that of making an un-unworthy character interesting in the eyes of the reader. Mr. Rochester is a man who deliberately and secretly seeks to violate the laws both of God and man, and yet we will be bound half our lady writers are enchanted with him for a model of generosity and honour."

We cannot, to-day, detect the " pedantry, stupidity, or gross vulgarity " of the novel ; nor do we distinguish so sharply between the sly governess —" this housemaid *beau ideal* of the arts of coquetry "—determined to catch Rochester, and the " noble, high-souled woman " who rejects his dishonourable proposals. The fact seems to be that masculine critics of those days regarded the *expression* of emotion as indelicate in woman. Was it this criticism, or merely her knowledge of men, that inspired that bitter passage in *Shirley* :

"A lover masculine if disappointed can speak and urge explanation ; a lover feminine can say nothing ; if she did, the result would be shame and anguish, inward remorse for self-treachery. Nature would brand such demonstration as a rebellion against her instincts, and would vindictively repay it afterwards by the thunderbolt of self-contempt smiting suddenly in secret. Take the matter as you find it ; ask no question ; utter no remonstrance : it is your best wisdom. You expected bread, and you have got a stone ; break your teeth on it, and don't shriek because the nerves are martyrised : do not doubt that your mental stomach—if you have such a thing—is strong as an ostrich's : the stone will digest. You held out your hand for an egg, and fate put into it a scorpion. Show no consternation : close your fingers firmly upon the gift ; let it sting through your palm. Never mind ; in time, after your hand and arm have swelled and quivered long with torture, the squeezed scorpion will die, and you will have learned the great lesson how to endure without a sob."

Men could not conceive that any lady who was *conscious* of love had " really nice feelings " about it. Moreover, Jane Eyre is " a mere heathen . . . no Christian grace is perceptible upon her." She upheld women's *rights*, which is " ungrateful " to God. " There is throughout a murmuring against the comforts of the rich and against the privations of the poor, which, as far as each individual is concerned, *is a murmuring against God's appointment."* Wherefore the " plain, odd woman, *destitute of all the conventional features of feminine attraction,"* is not made interesting, but

remains " a being totally uncongenial to our feelings
from beginning to end . . . a decidedly vulgar-
minded woman—one whom we should not care
for as an acquaintance, whom we should not seek
as a friend, whom we should not desire for a
relation, and whom we should most scrupulously
avoid for a governess."

This outspoken, and unsympathetic, criticism
is yet eminently instructive. It shows us all that
Charlotte Brontë accomplished for the first time ;
and reveals the full force of prejudice against
which she was, more or less consciously, in revolt.

It remains only to note that in the matter of
style her critics at once recognised her power. " It
is impossible not to be spellbound with the freedom
of the touch. It would be mere hackneyed
courtesy to call it ' fine writing.' It bears no
impress of being written at all, but is poured out
rather in the heat and flurry of an instinct which
flows ungovernably on to its object, indifferent by
what means it reaches it, and unconscious too."

Passing to modern criticism, we find one writer
declaring that Rochester's character " belongs
to the realm of the railway bookstall shilling
novel," while to another it seems " of all her

creations the most wonderful . . . from her own inmost nobility of temper and depth of suffering she moulded a man, reversing the marvels of God's creation."

It is not, I think, necessary to be dogmatic in comparing the "greatness" of *Villette* and *Jane Eyre*. The former is "more elaborated, more mature in execution, but less tragic, less simple and direct." The influence of personal tragedy (assuming her love for Monsieur Heger) obviously permeates the work; leading to the idealisation of the pedagogue genius (revived in Louis Gerard Moore, Esq.—himself half Flemish), and to unjust hostility against the Continental feminine (partially atoned for in Hortense Moore). On the other hand, it is more in touch with real life; less melodramatic, though still sensational; more acutely varied, and equally vivid, in characterisation.

Finally, in *Shirley*, if the spirit of Charlotte Brontë is less concentrated, it burns with no less steady flame. Here, for almost the first time in a woman-writer, we find that eager questioning upon the earlier struggles between capital and labour—the risks attendant upon the introduction of machinery, the proper relations between master and men—which afterwards became part of the stock material for fiction. We find, too, much shrewd comment upon her own experience of clerical types—no less in the contrast between Helstone and Hall than in the somewhat heavily satirised curates ; and some, probably inherited, injustice towards Dissenters. The characterisation is far more varied and more realistic ; since we have at least two pairs of lovers, the numerous Yorke family, and a whole host of " walking ladies and gentlemen," more or less carefully portrayed. Local colour appears in several passages of enthusiastic analysis of Yorkshire manners ; and the philosophy is frequently turned on everyday life. For example :

" In English country ladies there is this point to be remarked. Whether young or old, pretty or plain, dull or sprightly, they all (or almost all) have a certain expression stamped on their features, which seems to say, ' I know—I do not boast of it— but I *know* that I am the standard of what is proper ; let everyone therefore whom I approach, or who approaches me, keep a sharp look-out, for wherein they differ from me—be the same in dress, manner, opinion, principle, or practice — therein they are wrong."

Yet the inspiration of *Shirley* echoes *Jane Eyre* and *Villette*. Here, too, as we have seen,—though the heroine is a rich beauty,—Man should be Master ; and "indisputably, a great, good, handsome man is the first of created things." Yet neither Shirley nor her friend Caroline have anything in common with the "average" woman, who, "if her admirers only *told* her that she was an angel, would let them *treat* her like an idiot " ; or with her parents, who " would have delivered her over to the Rector's loving-kindness and his tender mercies without one scruple " ; or with the second Mrs. Helstone, who "reversing the natural order of insect existence, would have fluttered through the honeymoon, a bright, admired butterfly, and crawled the rest of her days a sordid, trampled worm."

Jane Eyre, 1847.
Shirley, 1849.
Villette, 1852.
The Professor, 1857.

"JANE EYRE" TO "SCENES OF CLERICAL LIFE"

(1847–1858)

EMILY BRONTË (1818–1848) can scarcely, in character or genius, be accommodated to any ordered consideration of development. Regarded by many enthusiasts as greater than her more famous sister, she stands alone for all time. Her one novel, *Wuthering Heights*, is unique for the passionate intensity of its emotions and the wild dreariness of its atmosphere. Save for the clumsily introduced stranger, who merely exists to "hear the story," the entire plot is woven about seven characters, all save one nearly related, and a few servants.

"Mr. Heathcliff," said the second Catherine, "*you* have *nobody* to love you ; and, however miserable you make us, we shall still have the revenge of thinking that your cruelty arises from your greater misery. You *are* miserable, are you not ? Lonely, like the devil, and envious like him ? *Nobody* loves you—*nobody* will cry for you when you die ! I wouldn't be you ! "

Charlotte calls him " child neither of Lascar nor gipsy, but a man's shape animated by demon life—a Ghoul—an afreet " ; and " from the time when ' the little black-haired swarthy thing, as dark as if it came from the Devil,' was first unrolled out of the bundle and set on its feet in the farm-house kitchen, to the hour when Nelly Dean found the grim, stalwart corpse laid on its back on the panel-enclosed bed, with wide-gazing eyes that seemed to ' sneer at her attempt to close them, and parted lips and sharp white teeth that sneered too,' " this human monster dominates every character and event in the whole book. Men and women, Linton or Earnshaw, are but pawns in his remorseless brain ; thwarting his will, daring his anger time after time ; yet always submitting at last to the will of their " master " : save, indeed, at the fall of the curtain, when he had " lost the faculty of enjoying destruction." For the passion of Heathcliff's strange existence is gloomy revenge—against fate and his own associates. Bitterly concentrated on the few human beings—all occupying two adjacent farms—with whom his life is passed, he seems the embodiment of an eternal curse, directed to thwart every natural feeling, every hope of happiness or peace.

Emily Brontë reveals no conception of humanity save this fiendish misanthrope ; churlish boors like Hindley and Hareton Earnshaw ; weak good people like Edgar, Isabella, and Linton ; passionate sprites like the two Catherines. Old Joseph indeed contains some elements of the comic spirit, exhibited in hypocrisy ; and Nelly Dean alone has *both* virtue and strength of character. But in making, or striving to unmake, marriages between these " opposites " ; in forcing their society upon each other, and hovering around his helpless victims ; the arch-fiend Heathcliff has ample scope for the indulgence of his diabolical whim. The tormenting of others and of himself ; the perverse making of misery for its own sake ; the ingenious exercise of brutal tyranny, are food and drink to this twisted soul. In ordinary cases we should wonder what might have happened had Catherine married him. We should set about picturing Heathcliff in happy possession of the love for which he craved so mightily : we should have murmured, " What cruel waste." But the power of Emily Brontë's conception denies us such idle imaginings. Heathcliff was manifestly incapable of " satisfaction " in anything, and there, as elsewhere, was Catherine his true mate. No circumstances, the most roseate or ideal, could have tamed his savage nature, quieted his stormy discontents, or lulled his passion for hurting all creatures weaker than himself. Such love as his must always have crushed and devoured what it yearned for : he could never have had enough of it · have rested in it, or rested upon it. He was, indeed, possessed by the " eighth devil."

In reality, then, the resemblance between Charlotte and Emily Brontë is comparatively superficial, arising from similarity of experience and the bleak atmosphere of the scenes and people among which they lived.[1] Emily can scarcely be called an exponent of human passion, since the beings she has created bear little or no resemblance to actual humanity.

[1] As Lockhart expresses it in the *Quarterly*, " There is a decided family likeness between *Jane Eyre* and *Wuthering Heights*, yet the aspect of the Jane and Rochester animals in their native state, as Catherine and Heathcliff, is too odiously and abominably pagan to be palatable even to the most vitiated class of novel readers. With all the unscrupulousness of the French school of novels it combines that repulsive vulgarity in the choice of its vice which supplies its own antidote."

Charlotte has told us that her sister's impressions
of scenery and locality are truthful, original, and
sympathetic ; the bleakness of the atmosphere is not
exaggerated. But, on the other hand, we learn —
as we should expect—that " she had scarcely more
practical knowledge of the peasantry among whom
she lived, than a nun has of the country people who
sometimes pass her gates. . . . She knew their
ways, their language, their family histories : she
could hear of them with interest, and talk of them
with detail, minute, graphic, and accurate ; but
with them she rarely exchanged a word." Hence,
having a naturally sombre mind, she drank in only
" those tragic and terrible traits of which, in
listening to the secret annals of every rude vicinage,
the memory is sometimes compelled to receive the
impress."

For those characteristics, more or less superficial,
in which her dramatis personæ resemble real life,
they are drawn, with marvellous insight and sympathy, from the moorlands ; but they are not, themselves, moorland folk. They are sheer creations
of the imagination. The terrible possibilities
which lurk within us are used indeed in the com-
pounding, but so combined and concentrated as

to banish all human semblance. It is up to any of us to become such as Heathcliff and the rest, for she has not violated the *possibilities* ; but a kinder fate, that grain of virtue and gentleness without which no human being was ever born and held his reason, has saved us from the absolutely elementary passions, tormenting and repining, of these strange beings.

She is as far from realism as an " unromantic " writer can well be ; and, by sheer force of will or vividness of imagination, compels and fascinates us to accept, as worthy of study and full of interest, the characters she has created.

And because, as has been often noticed, women are—curiously enough—not usually pre-eminent in imagination, her work remains supreme for certain qualities, which we may vainly seek elsewhere in English literature.

ANNE BRONTË (1820–1849) sheds but a pale glimmer beside her fiery sisters. She produced two novels : *Agnes Grey*, the record of a governess, and *The Tenant of Wildfell Hall*, a morbid picture of " talents misused and faculties abused "—both founded on personal experience. She worked quietly, but with mild resolution ; reproducing exactly her own observations on life, never straying beyond what she believed to be literally the truth. " She hated her work, but would pursue it. When reasoned with on the subject, she regarded such reasonings as a temptation to self-indulgence. She must be honest : she must not varnish, soften, or conceal."

Anne Brontë has left us her " warning " ; and if the stories embodying the moral are not particularly stimulating or dramatic, they do, after a pains-taking fashion, reveal character and reflect life. She had, moreover, a mild humour, entirely denied to Charlotte or Emily, as the following description of an " unchristian " rector may serve to show :

" Mr. Hatfield would come sailing up the aisle, or rather sweeping along like a whirlwind, with his rich silk gown flying behind him and rustling against the pew doors, mount the pulpit like a conqueror ascending his triumphal car ; then, sinking on the velvet cushion in an attitude of studied grace, remain in silent pros-tration for a certain time ; then mutter over a Collect, and gabble through the Lord's Prayer, rise, draw off one bright lavender glove, to give the congregation the benefit of his sparkling rings, lightly pass his fingers through his well-curled hair, flourish a cambric hand-kerchief, recite a very short passage, or, perhaps, a mere phrase of Scripture, as a headpiece to his discourse, and, finally, deliver a composition which, as a composition, might be considered good."

Like Charlotte, she prefers a plain heroine, seeming almost jealous of beauty in others, and regards man as the natural " master " of woman.

Art, inspired by a sense of duty, need not detain us further.

MRS. CRAIK (1826–1887) belongs, in all essentials, to the modern school of novelists ; although (like many another of her day) she appears almost more out-of-date than the women of genius who preceded her. For the " average " writers belong to one age and only one. Yet the enormous mass of work she produced may still be read with some pleasure, and deserves notice for its competent witness to certain phases of development in women's work.

In the first place she practically invented the " novel for the young person " (which is not " a children's story ") ; and, in the second, she carried to its extreme limit that enthusiasm for domestic sentimentality (which is quite different from " sensibility ") so dear to the Early Victorians.

Obviously it can be no matter for surprise that, as women became accustomed to the use of their pen and experienced in its influence, they should wake at last to the peculiar needs of their daughters —for a class of story which, without the false ideals of romance or the coarseness of early fiction, was in itself thoroughly interesting and absorbing. We have seen that, in purifying the novel, our greatest women-novelists were, for the most part, content to practise their art as an art. Jane Austen, undoubtedly, is a peculiarly wholesome writer (and therefore an influence for good) ; but she had no direct moral purpose.   And the didactic elements in Miss Edgeworth, Hannah More, and Harriet Martineau are somewhat inartistically pronounced.

In Mrs. Craik's day the desire for improvement was phenomenally active and varied.   She was " conscious " of this particular opening (afterwards expressed and developed by Miss Yonge), and, in her own manner, prepared to meet it.   It is impossible not to recognise that the whole appeal of *John Halifax, Gentleman* is directed towards youth.   The feminine idealism, whether applied to men or women, embraces all the vague and innocent dreams of heroic virtue which belong to the dawn of life.   The supreme domination of family life,

the education " at home " for boys and girls alike,
and a thousand other minutiæ of feeling and
opinion, are designed for that period—possibly
the most important in character-training—before
experience has tested the will.   There is no shirking
of truth, the method is realistic ; and we must
recognise the value of an atmosphere so refined
and purified, yet manly and practical.   For John
Halifax is always a fighter, one who makes his own
way—without sacrifice of principle or losing his
sympathy with the less capable, and less fortunate,
among the sons of toil.

John Halifax may fairly be taken as " standing "
for Mrs. Craik.   Here and in other novels (number-
ing about fifty) we may read her message, understand the Early Victorian lady, and observe one
groove along which the woman-novelist was destined
to work with comparative independence.   From
revealing themselves, they have turned (as had
Charlotte Brontë with very different results) to
give away their ideal of manhood.

MRS. OLIPHANT (1828–1897) belongs to the
same   group   of   thoroughly   efficient   Victorian
novelists as Mrs. Craik.   Living to an old age she

produced nearly a hundred volumes, all witnessing
the scope and power which had now been accepted
in women's work. Her output is far more varied
than Mrs. Craik's—bolder, more humorous, and
less sentimental. She published some admirable
history, a notable record of the Blackwoods—involving expert, if rather emotional, criticism—and
dabbled in the Unseen. Having great sympathy
with the Scotch temperament, she also imparted a
more modern tone to the " national " novel, somewhat after Galt's manner.

In her work also we find, very definitely, the
" note " of protest. Those truly feminine young
ladies (a Jane Austen pair), the daughters of the
Curate-in-Charge, for example, are perpetually in
revolt against convention. Mab, the artist, suffers
from a governess who considers drawing " unlady-
like," and believes that " a young lady who respects
herself, and who has been brought up as she ought,
never looks at gentlemen : There are drawings of
gentlemen in that book. Is that nice, do you
suppose ? " [1] The practical Cicely shoulders the
family burdens ; and is promptly " cut " by her

---

[1] " She did not approve of twilight walks. Why should
they want to go out just then like the tradespeople, a thing
which ladies never did."

friends, *because* she takes up the post of village schoolmistress. Like "John Halifax" she had been compelled to face life (for others as well as herself) with absolutely nothing but "her head and her hands." With less fuss she made an equally good fight, with no encouragement from that proud and tender-hearted old gentleman, her father, whose one idea of happiness was to "fall into our quiet way again." He "felt it was quite natural his girls should come home and keep house for him, and take the trouble of the little boys, and visit the schools : How is a man like that to be distinguished from a Dissenting preacher ? " To them it still seems : " We cannot go and do things like you men, and we feel all the sharper, all the keener, because we cannot *do*."

It is doubtful if women had ever been less conscious of their limitations, or less dissatisfied with them ; but the definite expression of criticism arose at this period, because they were acquiring the habit of expressing themselves, and had glimpses of possible change. From Charlotte Brontë, women not only pictured life from a feminine standpoint, but discussed and criticised it—a movement which " found itself " in George Eliot.

Mrs. Oliphant still speaks, and thinks, consciously, as a woman. But she does not " accept " everything. As to the craftmanship of fiction, we may now assume it for women, as had the public. We are reaching, indeed, the time when her province is no longer to stand aside. The later writers speak as individuals among artists, not as part of a group or school.

As mentioned above, Mrs. Oliphant also wrote competent criticism and played the part, still comparatively novel among women, of an all-round practical journalist, knowing the world of letters, familiar with publishers and the " business " of authorship, handling history or biography like a person of culture. In her later years she essayed, in *The Beleaguered City* and elsewhere, some way into that field of psychic inquiry—developed by her son Laurence—and since their day a familiar topic in fiction.

At one time, indeed, greater things were expected of her. *The Chronicles of Carlingford* (1863) approach genius. They appeared after *Adam Bede*, and it is scarcely surprising that men imagined the discovery of a second George Eliot. We find in them that almost masculine insight—

from an intellectual eminence—of parochial affairs, small society, and the country town, combined with passionate character-analysis, emotional philosophy, and bracing humour, which constituted the individuality of George Eliot.

Mrs. Oliphant, in her early days, produced several " Chronicles," in which the characters re-appear, though diversely centralised ; and we may consider two examples at some length.

Miss Marjoribanks, following the woman's lead, is professedly a study in a certain feminine type. The heroine was known among her schoolfellows as " a large girl."

" She was not to be described as a tall girl—which conveys an altogether different idea—but she was large in all particulars, full and well-developed, with somewhat large features, not at all pretty as yet, though it was known in Mount Pleasant that somebody had said that such a face might ripen into beauty, and become ' grandiose,' for anything anybody could tell. Miss Marjoribanks was not vain ; but the word had taken possession of her imagination, as was natural, and solaced her much when she made the painful discovery that her gloves were half a number larger, and her shoes a hair-breadth broader, than those of any of her companions ; but the hands and feet were perfectly well-shaped ; and being at the same time well-clothed and plump, were much more presentable and pleasant to look upon than the lean rudimentary school-girl hands with which they were surrounded. To add to these excellences, Lucilla had a mass of hair which, if it could but have been cleared a little in its tint, would have been golden, though at present it was nothing more than tawny, and curly to exasperation. She wore it in large thick curls, which did not, however, float or wave, or do any of the graceful things which curls ought to do ; for it had this aggravating quality, that it would not grow long, but would grow ridiculously, unmanageably thick, to the admiration of her companions, but to her own despair, for there was no knowing what to do with those short but ponderous locks."

After which unconventional description, we are not surprised to learn that our heroine " was possessed by nature of that kind of egotism, or rather egoism, which is predestined to impress itself, by its perfect reality and good faith, upon the surrounding world. . . . This conviction of the importance and value of her own proceedings made Lucilla, as she grew older, a copious and amusing conversationalist—a rank which few people who are indifferent to, or do not believe in, themselves can attain to."

Miss Marjoribanks had two objects in life—to " be a comfort to " her widowed father and

"to revolutionise society." Undoubtedly she
" made " Carlingford, and, though her father was
perfectly satisfied with his own management of life,
she did actually succeed in proving herself essential to his well-being. A young woman who, on
her own showing, " never made mistakes " and
was " different " from other ladies, was able to
effect much with the " very good elements " of
Carlingford. She created a social atmosphere of
peculiar distinction, she managed the most in-
tractable of archdeacons, she found " the right
man " to represent the borough. She was as
fearless as, and far more successful than, Miss
Woodhouse, in making marriages ; and in every
respect went her own way with a most engaging
self-confidence. Dr. Marjoribanks respected and
" understood " her, though he thought her more
" worldly " than she proved herself ; and no one
gave her full credit " for that perfect truthfulness
which it was her luck always to be able to main-
tain."

The character is worth our study ; for it is
improbable that fiction has ever produced, or will
ever venture to repeat, a heroine so entirely convinced of a mission in life, and so competent to

carry it out. Scarcely ever concerned with sentiment, she had a genius for doing " the right thing,"
and thoroughly enjoying the contemplation of
her own achievements. Yet she was really generous and kind-hearted, entirely above jealousy or
meanness. We may question, perhaps, whether
any woman, or man either, was ever quite so consistent : since even in yielding to Cousin Tom's
importunities, she was but planning a new campaign—" to carry light and progress " into " the
County." Yet few readers will fail to recognise
the power and charm of Lucilla Marjoribanks—
a new revelation of what a woman conceives woman
may be.

In all her dialogue, in the narrative, and in the
minor characterisation, Mrs. Oliphant here proves
herself an easy master of convincing realism. We
know Carlingford and its inhabitants as intimately
as our native town.

Salem Chapel, indeed, reveals another side
of the picture. Miss Marjoribanks and her friends
were staunch church people. The sturdy deacons,
their women-folk, and Mr. Vincent's whole flock,
belong to another sphere. " Greengrocers, dealers
in cheese and bacon, milkmen, with some dress-

makers of inferior pretensions, and teachers of day
schools of similar humble character, formed the
élite of the congregation." Indeed, " the young
man from 'Omerton " proves to be something of
a firebrand among these simple souls. His declaration of independence does not meet with their
approval : " Them ain't the sentiments for a
pastor in our connection. That's a style of thing
as may do among fine folks, or in the church where
there's no freedom ; but them as chooses their
own pastor, and don't spare no pains to make
him comfortable, has a right to expect different."
Since the poor fellow is " getting his livin' off
them all the time," he must go their way without
question : " A minister ain't got no right to have
business of his own, leastways on Sundays. Preaching's his business." The most loyal of them can
always recall " that period of delightful excitation
when they were hearing candidates, and felt themselves the dispensers of patronage " ; though, as
the caustic Adelaide truthfully remarked, " even
when they are asses like your Salem people, you
know they like a man with brains " ; and Mr.
Vincent had " filled the chapel."

Mrs. Oliphant has contrasted the limitations of

Dissent with a somewhat melodramatic personal tragedy which insensibly draws Mr. Vincent under the influence of " them great ladies " who " when they're pretty-looking " are " no better nor evil spirits," and, alas, " a minister of our connection as was well acquainted with them sort of folks would be out of nature." The whole atmosphere is obviously uncongenial, and we see that it makes the man totally unfit for his work.

Nevertheless, it is with two characters wholly " within the fold " that our sympathies must finally remain. It is Mrs. Vincent and Tozer the Butter-man who are the real hero and heroine. Certainly the gentle widow cannot understand her clever son, and her absolute lack of common sense is quite exasperating ; but everyone recognises that she is " quite the lady," and no Roman mother of classic immortality ever revealed such perfect loyalty under such tragic difficulties. She knew " how little a thing makes mischief in a congregation," for " she had been a minister's wife for thirty years," and her superb devotion to doing the right thing by everybody conquered persons of far greater intellect and assurance, under difficulties that few men could have faced

for any consideration. Again and again this quiet
and most provokingly fussy of women absolutely
dominates the stage, conquering all adversaries.
She is almost absurdly inadequate for the "realities"
of life ; but such a past mistress of tact and
decorum, so instinctively aware of " what is expected of her," and so courageously punctilious
in manner, that she triumphs over odds the most
overwhelming, proving inflexible where she knows
her ground. Entirely without control over her
emotions, she yet never forgets or fails in her
" duty."

The heroism of Mr. Tozer, naturally, does not
depend upon such subtleties or refinements. He
is of sterner stuff ; but it would be hard to find, in
life or fiction, a zealous deacon, so thoroughly
conversant with the duties and the privileges of
his position, who could rise with such broad-
minded charity to circumstances so exceptional.
He is genuinely kind, and really loyal to Mr.
Vincent. Without the slightest knowledge, or any
power to appreciate the emotional turmoil which
had thrown that young minister off his balance,
the worthy shopkeeper trusts his own instincts,
fights like a hero for his friend, and absolutely

pulverises the enemy. He has no natural gifts for eloquence, no diplomacy or tact ; but he has faith, insight, and courage.

The minister's wife and the deacon entirely remove the reproach we might otherwise level against Mrs. Oliphant of satirical contempt for Nonconformity. With Miss Marjoribanks, they establish her power in characterisation.

Finally, the crowded picture of life at Carlingford given in the two novels prepares us for that conscious and professional study of " material " for fiction which women had only recently acquired, and which bears its finest fruit in George Eliot.

CHARLOTTE M. YONGE (1823–1901) presents almost as many facets as Mrs. Oliphant, but her work more nearly resembles Mrs. Craik's. Primarily a High-Churchwoman and a sentimentalist, she was more directly educational than either. Her *Cameos of English History* are models of popular narrative, a little coloured by prejudice ; but no praise can be too high for that children's story, also historical, *The Little Duke,* or for the equally charming *The Lances of Lynwood.*

As a novelist she was chiefly concerned, as hinted

already, with the *conscious* development of the tale
" for the young person," which she defines and
justifies in her

PREFACE TO " THE DAISY CHAIN ; OR, ASPIRATIONS "

" No one can be more sensible than is the author
that the present is an overgrown book of a nondescript
class, neither the ' tale ' for the young, nor the novel
for their elders, but a mixture of both.

" Begun as a series of conversational sketches, the
story outran both the original intention and the limits
of the periodical in which it was commenced ; and,
such as it has become, it is here presented to those
who have already made acquaintance with the May
family, and may be willing to see more of them. It
would beg to be considered merely as what it calls
itself, a Family Chronicle—a domestic record of home
events, large and small, during those years of early
life when the character is chiefly formed, and as an
endeavour to trace the effects of those aspirations
which are a part of every youthful nature. That the
young should take the hint, to think whether their
hopes and upward breathings are truly upwards, and
founded in lowliness, may be called the moral of the
tale.

" For those who may deem the story too long, and
the characters too numerous, the author can only beg
their pardon for any tedium that they may have
undergone before giving it up.

" Feb. 22nd, 1856."

As it happens, this passage contains several points which serve to elucidate the special characteristics of its author's work. We see at once the serious moral purpose, and its direct aim. We may notice, again, that she at least recognises, and admits, what may be called disparagingly the chief function of women novelists—the narration of "Family Chronicles," the domesticity, the emphasis on "home" life. And, finally, we have a confession of her tendency to overcrowd the characters; her devotion for persons to whom the reader has been already introduced, now reappearing—for further development—in another tale.

Miss Yonge, in fact, had a weakness for genealogy. One novel often describes the children of persons figuring in another. We may recognise old friends in every chapter. No doubt the habit may become wearisome, and it was carried to excess. But, on the other hand, we must be conscious of exceptional familiarity with "the May family," for example; and the process, when restrained with discretion, is a perfectly legitimate application of the realistic ideal. In real life the plots are not rounded off in one volume. Reunions that are utterly unexpected, if not unwelcome, are constantly surprising

us, and the children of friends or relatives have a
natural bias towards each other.

Moreover, in this matter Miss Yonge reveals
extraordinary skill. Technically, we could name the
heroine of *The Daisy Chain*. She has several peculiarities, recalling Maggie Tulliver. But we are nearly
as intimate with the two Margarets ; the " worldly "
sister is drawn with subtle command of detail ; the
innumerable brothers are perfectly differentiated ;
Dr. May stands out clear in every mood ; the
" heiress " is absolutely alive ; and there is no hesitation about the minor characters. Miss Yonge can
' manage" as many people as you please. There is
no faltering or hesitation about her touch anywhere.

To-day, probably, we do not quite willingly
accept so much religiosity. We certainly cannot
" assume " the Church. Our " aspirations " may
not expend themselves upon a steeple or a Sunday
school. But there can be no question about this
good lady's understanding of young people. The
family picture is sound and wholesome. No member of the group offends us by his or her sancti-
monious perfection. All are perfectly human,
youthfully impulsive, and wholesomely eager.
And the Early Victorians *were* sentimental.

As in *John Halifax, Gentleman*, the atmosphere belongs to the dawn of life. The love-stories—of which, needless to say, we have several—are whole-hearted, without complexity. There is no juggling with right and wrong, no " questioning," no element of sordidness.

Though we should alter a good deal, perhaps, in detail—of manner, thought, and ideal—it is difficult to see how work could be done better for the particular class of readers appealed to ; who would, undoubtedly, actually prefer a crowd.

Once more, Miss Yonge is frankly feminine. She has established one more special function for women novelists, a legitimate offspring of the domestic realism which they followed from the first; a work almost impossible to man.

A PROFESSIONAL WOMAN

(George Eliot, 1819–1880)

George Eliot once declared that " if art does
not enlarge men's sympathies, it does nothing
morally. . . . The only effect I long to produce by
my writings is that those who read them shall
be better able to *imagine* and to *feel* the pains
and joys of those who differ from themselves."

It is written in *Adam Bede* :

" My strongest effort is to avoid any arbitrary
picture, and to give a faithful account of men and
things as they have mirrored themselves in my mind.
The mirror is doubtless defective ; the outlines will
sometimes be disturbed, the reflection faint or confused ;
but I feel *as much bound* to tell you as precisely as I
can what that reflection is, *as if I were in a witness box
narrating my experience on oath.* . . .

" I would not, even if I had the choice, be the clever
novelist who could create a world so much better than
this, in which we get up in the morning to do our daily
work, that you would be likely to turn a harder, colder
eye on the dusty streets and the common green fields
—on the real breathing men and women who can be

chilled by your indifference or injured by your prejudice, who can be cheered and helped onward by your
fellow-feeling, your forbearance, your outspoken, brave
justice.

" So I am content to tell my simple story, without
trying to make things seem better than they were ;
dreading nothing, indeed, but falsity, which, in spite
of one's efforts, there is reason to dread. Falsehood
is so easy, truth so difficult. . . .

" It is for this rare, precious quality of truthfulness
that I delight in many Dutch paintings ; which lofty-
minded people despise. I find a source of delicious
sympathy in these faithful pictures of a monotonous,
homely existence, which has been the fate of so many
more among my fellow-mortals than a life of pomp
or of absolute indigence, of tragic suffering or of world-
stirring actions. I turn, without shrinking, from cloud-
borne angels, from prophets, sibyls, and heroic warriors,
to an old woman bending over her flower-pot, or eating
her solitary dinner, while the noonday light, softened
perhaps by a screen of leaves, falls on her mob-cap, and
just touches the rim of her spinning wheel, and her
stone jug, and all those cheap common things which
are the precious necessaries of life to her ; or I turn
to that village wedding, kept between four brown
walls, where an awkward bridegroom opens the dance
with a high-shouldered, broad-faced bride, while
elderly and middle-aged friends look on, with very
irregular noses and lips, and probably with quart-pots
in their hands, but with an expression of unmistakable
contentment and good-will. . . .

" All honour and reverence to the divine beauty of
form ! Let us cultivate it to the utmost in men,
women, and children—in our gardens and in our houses.
. . . Paint us an angel if you can, with a floating
violet robe, and a face paled by the celestial light ;
paint us yet oftener a Madonna, turning her mild face
upward and opening her arms to welcome the divine
glory ; but do not impose on us any æsthetic rules which
shall banish from the region of art those old women
scraping carrots with their work-worn hands, those
heavy clowns taking holiday in a dingy pothouse,
those rounded backs and stupid, weather-worn faces
that have bent over the spade and done the rough
work of the world—those homes with their tin pans,
their brown pitchers, their rough curs, and their clusters
of onions. . . .

" There are few prophets in the world, few sublimely
beautiful women, few heroes. I can't afford to give
all my love and reverence to such rarities : I want
a great deal of those feelings for my everyday fellow-
men, especially for the few in the foreground of the
great multitude whose faces I know, whose hands I
touch, for whom I have to make way with kindly
courtesy. Neither are picturesque lazzaroni or romantic
criminals half so frequent as your common labourer,
who gets his own bread, and eats it vulgarly but credit-
ably with his own pocket-knife. It is more needful
that I should have a fibre of sympathy connecting
me with that vulgar citizen who weighs out my sugar
in a vilely-assorted cravat and waistcoat, than with
the handsomest rascal in red scarf and green feathers ;

more needful that my heart should swell with loving admiration at some trait of gentle goodness in the faulty people who sit at the same hearth with me, or in the clergyman of my own parish, who is perhaps rather too corpulent, and in other respects is not an Oberlin or a Tillotson, than at the deeds of heroes whom I shall never know except by hearsay, or at the sublimest abstract of all clerical graces that was ever conceived by an able novelist."

Woman has found, and proclaimed, her mission. She is a moral realist, and her realism is not inspired by any idle ideal of art, but by sympathy with life. Jane Austen and Mary Mitford were compared, condescendingly, with Dutch painters. George Eliot claims the parallel with pride. It may be questioned if realism was ever defended with so much eloquence, from such high motives. Finally, if the romance of high life has no place in these pictures, neither has the romance of crime, adventure, or squalid destitution. They hold up the mirror to mediocrity. They present the parish.

And for many years George Eliot influenced thought and culture among the middle-classes more widely, and perhaps more profoundly, than any other writer. We can remember a generation for whom the moral problems involved in the relations between Dorothea and Will Ladislaw were a favourite topic for tea-table conversation in serious families; and when the novelist herself married a second time, it seemed to many that an ideal had been desecrated. Her intensity of religious feeling, combined with independence towards theological authority, expressed with truly artistic effect the whole temperament of an age whose spiritual cravings were almost exclusively ethical. Her contribution to literature, placing her in the highest rank, was the creation of many characters, instinct with humanity, struggling with fine moral earnestness towards the attainment of an ideal, halting long and stumbling often by the way. Their appeal to young readers of each generation is irresistible; while the crowded backgrounds, so truthfully and dramatically portrayed, of a day when the English middle-classes were ever eager in extending their moral and mental horizon, can never lose value as an important chapter in social history.

If we have read them rightly, it is this for which women's work had been all along preparing the way. George Eliot certainly had not so great a genius as Jane Austen or Charlotte Brontë ; she was not a pioneer like Fanny Burney. But she had greater breadth, more firm solidity ; and she was conscious of her aim, with the professional training, the culture, *and* the genius to achieve.

Women, we see, have been always realistic and parochial. They have avoided the glitter of wealth and the grime of sin. Tender to prodigals, they have loved the home. If the " intense and continuous note of personal conviction," so conspicuous in George Eliot, began with Charlotte Brontë, women have always felt and thought morally.

She has been summarily dismissed as an " example of the way in which the novel—once a light and frivolous thing—had come to be taken with the utmost seriousness—had in fact ceased to be light literature at all, and began to require rigorous and elaborate training and preparation in the writer, perhaps even something of the athlete's processes in the reader."

But such seriousness was characteristic of her age, and everyone had then learnt to demand professionalism in art ; while, on the other hand, readers of 1821 were assured that " Miss Austen had the merit of being evidently a Christian writer,"

who conveyed " that unpretending kind of instruction which is furnished by real life," and whose
works may " on the whole be recommended, not
only as among the most unexceptionable of their
kind, but as combining, in an eminent degree,
instruction with amusement."

Charlotte Brontë, we may remember, was declared, by her contemporaries, " one who has, for
some sufficient reason, long forfeited the society of
her sex " ; and George Eliot herself was accused
of " coarseness and immorality," in her attempt
" to familiarise the minds of our young women
in the middle and higher ranks with matters on
which their fathers and brothers would never
venture to speak in their presence . . . and to
intrude on minds which ought to be guarded from
impurity the unnecessary knowledge of evil." To
such critics her claim to kinship with the " honest
old Dutchman " is set aside for a parallel to " the
perverseness of our modern ' pre-Raphaelites,' with
their choice of disagreeable subjects, uncomely
models, and uncouth attitudes."

Such is the natural result of women daring to
think for themselves. To-day we are content
rather to notice that Miss Burney first cleansed the

circulating library, and Miss Austen most un-
obtrusively extolled the domestic virtues ; while
their sisters in art all contributed to the prevalence
of wholesome fiction ; until Miss Brontë and George
Eliot stirred up the conscience of man towards
woman. In reality women are born preachers, and
always work for an ideal.

The period, indeed, is already approaching in
which women's work can no longer be treated
en masse and by itself, apart from men's. It is no
longer essentially spontaneous or unconscious, as
in Miss Burney and Jane Austen. We have described the writers immediately preceding George
Eliot as professional experts, careful of art ; and
once the world had learnt to *expect* good work from
woman and grown accustomed to her as an artist,
there remained no further occasion for her to speak
as a woman among aliens. George Eliot, indeed,
like Charlotte Brontë, had been, by some of her
contemporaries, taken for a man ; but the youngest
and most inexperienced reader to-day could scarcely
have been momentarily deceived. There are, indeed, certain tricks, or mannerisms, of masculinity ;
but they are superficial, and not actually worn
with much grace or skill.

No earlier woman-writer, indeed, had assumed so comprehensive a philosophy, or scarcely any attempt at ordered opinion on life in general, on character, or on faith. But, despite the enthusiasm of certain biographers, despite the influence—unquestioned—of Herbert Spencer, Strauss, George Henry Lewes, and others, we are not personally disposed to grant much weight to our author's generalisations ; while certainly the obtrusiveness of her moralising is an artistic blemish.

The fact is that George Eliot's outlook remains thoroughly emotional and feminine. In herself, we know, she always saw life through a man-interpreter ; and the didactics of her novels are derived from the study of books, not from the exercise of independent reason or thought. If she *talked* ethics, she *felt* faith.

But, on the other hand, her work has little external affinity with that of the women of genius preceding her (though it may be a natural development from theirs), because it is obviously the result of training and study, that is *professional*. It is, moreover, the first important contribution by women to the problem novel with a purpose. Both

points can be easily illustrated by the most
elementary comparison.

We have tacitly assumed, and with obvious
justification in fact, that Fanny Burney and Jane
Austen, for example, wrote entirely out of their
own personal experience. We picture their own
surroundings from the society in their novels,
noting the power acquired by the limitation.
Charlotte Brontë did not go beyond her own circle,
save in imagination. But George Eliot, no less
certainly, *studied* mankind *for copy*. It is true
that she made more direct *use of* her own family
and friends than they. Maggie Tulliver is no less
autobiographical than Lucy Snowe. True also that
for description and atmosphere she depended largely
on memory. But even here the treatment is that
of a self-conscious artist, composing and presenting
from outside, studying effects, grouping types;
always alive to a comparison between life and
literature. And as she *uses* the human material
which has come to her in the natural order of things,
she increases it by the journalist's eye for new copy,
piquant contrast, and unexpected revelation. She
invokes, moreover, the assistance of every literary
device—prepared humour, scholarly style, cultured

allusion, local colour, analytical characterisation, and dramatic construction. We have here no longer a spontaneous revelation of woman ; rather her captain in full array, armed for fight.

Nor is the message, or open discussion of problems, less novel or less deliberate. It was possible, indeed inevitable, to notice in the earlier examples of woman's work that she held theories on life not quite in accord with what man had always expected from her. Part of her inspiration, no doubt, was the desire to express these. On certain points, recognised womanly,—such as education and the ordering of a home,—she soon learnt to speak openly ; but, in the main, we studied the woman's ideal of character and conduct from her portrait-painting ; we deduced her approval from her sympathy, her budding criticism from her scorn. If she attempted direct teaching, it was mostly in support of mere conventional duty ; the reward of virtue and the punishment of vice, tentatively measured perhaps by a standard, not quite blindly copied from men. The greatest artists among women before Charlotte Brontë never obtruded the moral, discussed the problem.

But what was fearlessly urged on a few chosen

topics from the Haworth parsonage became the
foreground and main subject with the assistant
editor of the *Westminster Review*. We are, to-
day, somewhat overweighted with problem novels ;
but George Eliot was the first among us to realise
the full power of fiction as a vehicle more per-
suasive, if not more powerful, than the pulpit ;
for the fearless and intimate discussion of all the
questions and difficulties which must confront a
man, or a woman, who is not content to accept
things as they are, or to believe all he is told.
To-day we may detect

" a curious *naïveté* in the whole impression George
Eliot's novels convey. . . . The ethical law is, in her
universe, as all powerful as the law of gravitation, and as
unavoidable. Remorse, degeneration of character, and
even material loss, are meted out for transmission with
the rigid and childlike sense of justice which animated
the writers of the Old Testament. Her temper was
Hebraistic, and goodness was more to her than beauty.
It may be doubted whether in the world, as we see it,
justice works as impartially and with such unmistakable exactitude, whether the righteous is never forsaken, and evil always hunts the wicked person to
overthrow him."

But we must remember that George Eliot's
conception of wickedness, if limited, was well in

advance of her age ; that she understood temptation, and could draw a most dramatically " mixed "
character. Her people are not all black or all
white. She knew how slight an error or slip, how
amiable a weakness, could lead to actions which
the Pharisee called sin, and the Puritan would
punish with hell-fire. She entirely forgave Maggie
Tulliver, she held out the hand of fellowship to
Godfrey Cass, and even to Arthur Donnithorne.
If " we are almost afraid of " Dinah Morris, she,
too, certainly loved sinners. George Eliot, in fact,
will not accept any opinion on authority, or follow
the world in judgment ; and if " the world has
never produced a woman philosopher," her work
remains pre-eminent as the first complete and
outspoken record of woman's " scientific speculation to discover an interpretation of the universe,"
her first conscious message to mankind ; destined
to " raise the standard of prose-fiction to a higher
power ; to give it a new impulse and motive."
She has now spoken for herself on conduct and
on faith.

Nevertheless George Eliot remains a woman.
We still look to her primarily for the revelation
of woman, and woman's vision of man. We have

taken another step, onward and inward, towards
the mystery of the feminine ideal, the meaning of
the Home and the Family to those who make it.
All this is far more complex, indeed, than anything
we have studied in earlier chapters. It embraces,
in *Romola*, some reconstruction of past times ;
in *Daniel Deronda*, some study of an alien race.
It includes sympathy for a woman wandering so
far from the natural feminine instincts as to
abandon, and half murder, her own child ; for a
girl who, given to dreamy ideals and passionate
self-sacrifice, will yet suffer attentions from the
acknowledged lover of her cousin, simply because
he is handsome. It reveals the genuine repentance and uplifting of a drunken wife ; it permits
" friendship " between a married woman and a
young artist whose very vices are more attractive
than the heartless tyrannical egoism of her
husband. We have travelled a long way, certainly, from Catherine Morland and Fanny Price.
We can imagine a new Lydia Bennet under George
Eliot.

  Still the problems are women's problems : the
solutions are feminine, as we may see from the
eagerness with which they were condemned by

man, the conservative and the conventional.
" I'm no denyin'," said Mrs. Poyser, " the women
are foolish. God almighty made 'em to match
the men." It was George Eliot's ambition, towards
which she accomplished much, that " the women "
should be less intent upon that *matching*, more
willing, and able, to mould themselves after their
own pattern : in their turn to form a creed, to
establish a standard—wherein she was following,
but more consciously, those who had gone before.
As Huxley remarked, in answer to Princess Louise,
she did not " go in for " the superiority of women.
She rather " *teaches the inferiority of men.*"

For, verily, there is no more in it. Her women
are lost outside the home ; they are not financi-
ally, or intellectually, " independent." They
have no professions, no clubs, no sports. Their
interests are confined to religion, domesticity,
and love. Nor does George Eliot attempt to
follow " the men " into politics [1] or business, on
to the cricket field or the parade ground. A
soldier is distinguished by his regimentals, a
scholar by his library, a doctor by his gig. She
has a strong partiality, tempered by criticism,

---

[1] *Felix Holt* is a possible, but not a successful, exception.

for the clergy ; she can distinguish, intelligently, between Church and Dissent ; she knows a good deal about squires and farmers ; she loves the labourer. We may safely regard her work as the continuation, and the completion, of our subject.

The completion, indeed, is rather intellectual than artistic. She covers the whole ground, as none of her predecessors had attempted ; she makes the last final addition of subject by discovering, and facing, social problems ; she applies the last word in literary professionalism ; but inasmuch as her characters are more typical and more studied than Jane Austen's, they are, in a sense, less modern and less universal. We may learn *more* from her about women, and women's opinions ; but these are the women of one age only—fast awakening, indeed, and conscious of many troubling possibilities, but not free.

Their chief aim is, while widening their knowledge and sympathy, to speak with imperious accents of duty, that " stern Daughter of the Voice of God." Despite her assumption of masculine logic and reasoning, itself an artistic blemish, she offers no explanation of her categorical and materialistic, ethical dogma. The distinction between good

and evil with her is in the last resort a question
of emotional instinct, haunted by " the faltering
hope that a spiritual interpretation of the universe may be true." It is impossible to avoid
feeling that she accords the greatest strength of
character to serene piety like that of Dinah Morris,
or to Adam Bede's conception of the " deep, spiritual
things in religion . . . when feelings come into
you like a rushing, mighty wind. . . . His work,
as you know, had always been part of his religion,
and from very early days he saw clearly that good
carpentry was God's will." In her heart of hearts,
George Eliot, we are certain, would have echoed
Mrs. Poyser's preference for character over doctrine : " Mr. Irvine was like a good meal o' victual,
you were the better for him without thinking on it ;
and Mr. Ryde was like a dose o' physic, he gripped
you and worrited you, and, after all, he left you
much the same."

It was Mr. Irvine, you will remember, who put
on his slippers before going upstairs to his plain,
invalid sister ; and " whoever remembers how
many things he has declined to do even for himself,
rather than have the trouble of putting on or
taking off his boots, will not think this last detail

insignificant." It needs a woman, however, to appreciate such a service of love.

George Eliot, indeed, could be humorous, some-what pedantically, and even genial about little things, and she recognised most fully their import-ance in life. But her more calculated and accumu-lative effects were all tragic or subdued melancholy ; partly, no doubt, from this uncertainty of hers about faith and her passionate sense of justice, so relent-less in its demand for the punishment of sin ; partly also from that tinge of sadness which overshadows the narrow, old-fashioned dogma by which her own childhood was moulded. Hard as she strove for intellectual freedom, and eagerly as she proclaimed independence of judgment, the halter of early im-pressions was round her neck ; and it is only by dwelling upon incidents or individuals, and ignoring the studied main motive, that we can gain from her work any of the joy in physical or natural beauty which should be an artist's first care to impart.

Yet, after all, nature has triumphed over tem-perament. In reality, for example, Dinah Morris lives for us in her tactful tenderness for the queru-lous old Lisbeth, and in her yearning towards Hetty ;

not in the " call," the " leading," and the " voices "
by which her ministry was inspired.   On the other
hand, we admire her dignified superiority to masculine criticism of women's preaching : " It isn't
for men to make channels for God's Spirit, as they
make channels for the water-courses, and say, ' Flow
here, but flow not there.' "

Hetty Sorrel, again, was only adventurous
through misfortune ; she belongs to the fireside.
Dorothea was a hero-worshipper ; Maggie Tulliver
is the ideal sister ; Mary Garth the ideal helpmate.
The crimes of Rosamond Vincy, if there be no mercy
in their exposure, are wholly domestic ; the sins
of Janet are committed for her husband.

It is the same with the men.   Amos Barton is
only a poor country clergyman, and grey-haired
Mr. Gilfil " filled his pocket with sugar-plums for
the little children."   Adam Bede " had no theories
about setting the world to rights," and " couldn't
abide a fellow who thought he made himself fine
by being coxy to's betters."   The Tullivers, father
and son, were, in their different ways, as fine speci-
mens of honest tradesmen as Bulstrode was a con-
summate hypocrite of the provinces.   Lydgate
was no more than an exceptionally clever and

cultured general practitioner, and we fancy that Will Ladislaw was a better lover than artist.   George Eliot's squires are typical ornaments of the country-side ; her farmers belong as permanently to one side of the hearth as their wives to the other.   Silas Marner, practising a trade that could not " be carried on entirely without the help of the Evil One," since " all cleverness was in itself suspicious," had no power of filling his life with " movement, mental activity, and close fellowship " outside the " narrow religious sect " in which his youth was passed.

Nancy Osgood " actually said ' mate ' for 'meat,' ' 'appen ' for ' perhaps,' and ' 'oss ' for ' horse,' which, to young ladies living in good Lytherly society, who habitually said 'orse, even in domestic privacy, and only said 'appen on the right occasions, was necessarily shocking." She supported " a cheerful face under rough answers and unfeeling words by the belief that ' a man must have so much on his mind ' " ; and " had her unalterable code " ready for all occasions.

They are not an heroic company, you perceive, these sons and daughters of a highly intellectual woman-novelist.   In its more primitive exponents their " kindness " is " of a beery and bungling

sort," their anger is brutal and bigoted ; they are
not really interested in general principles, in psychological analysis, in refined passion, or in the future
of mankind. Yet they are very serious about life,
a good deal puzzled by the apparent injustice of
God, and filled with love or hatred towards all
their neighbours. In this parish, as in most,
everyone knows all about everyone else's affairs,
and finds them of supreme interest.

Thus George Eliot maintains the feminine attention to minutiæ ; the woman's centralisation of
Life round the family. She has acquired knowledge, " read up " literature, and to some extent
digested philosophy ; but she applies her powers,
her culture, and her training—from practice and
association with professional writers—to the ampli-
fication and rounding off of woman's art. She
established domestic realism by the expression of
feminine insight. She is content to leave other
things to other pens. The appearance of generalisations not influenced by her sex is misleading. It is
only a modern form of the old story. Her heart,
and her genius, are those of a woman, womanly.

Scenes of Clerical Life, 1858.
Adam Bede, 1859.

The Mill on the Floss, 1860.
Silas Marner, 1861.
Romola, 1863.
Felix Holt, 1866.
Middlemarch, 1872.
Daniel Deronda, 1876.

THE GREAT FOUR

BEFORE completing our general conclusions as to the aim and achievement of women's work, it may be well to institute certain comparisons between the four writers of genius around whom we have chronicled our record of progress; to estimate the ground covered by their work; to analyse their ideals, witnessing change and development.

Although, as we have seen, all primarily domestic, if not actually parochial, the middle-class, " set " as a subject by Richardson, became—more or less consciously—subdivided in their hands. Fanny Burney confined herself, almost without reserve, to studies of town life, with an occasional digression to fashionable health resorts. It is true that her heroines may sigh for a sylvan glade or dream of green fields : no woman of sensibility could do less. In their minds the country must inevitably be allied to virtue and content. But we cannot pretend that the rural scenes of *Camilla* are drawn from nature ; and Miss Burney was, undoubtedly, most at home in the drawing-room, at the assembly,

in the opera-house, or at the baths. Nowhere
else can we find so vivid and lifelike a picture of
Society in the eighteenth century—the dramatic
contrast with "Commerce at play" recalling
Vanity Fair. It is here, in fact, that Miss Burney's
exceptional personal experience gave her the
enviable opportunity of drawing both Mayfair and
Holborn at first hand. She is specifically Metro-
politan, though we should not say Cockney. In
her imagination there is no world outside London,
no higher ambition than notoriety about Town.

The difference in Jane Austen's work is almost
startling. She seems practically unaware of
London ; and it would be difficult to name any
group of intelligent persons so absolutely indifferent
to its gaieties, its activities, or its problems as the
characters in *all* her novels. It may be that Lucy
Steele could not so easily have caught Robert
Ferrars elsewhere ; but the few Town chapters in
Sense and Sensibility only illustrate our contention
as a whole, since the relations between all remain
precisely the same as in the country, and practically
everyone is delighted to "get away again." The
John Knightleys and the excellent Gardiners,
indeed, live in London : but we only meet them

away from home ; and, after all, the one " suggestive " comment on town life is the " unexpected
discovery " that people who " live over their
business " were able to " mix with " the County.

Jane Austen's familiars are all drawn from the
most unpromising circle : those who live " just
outside " small towns, have just enough to live on
without working for it, are just sufficiently well-
bred to marry into " the County," just simple
enough to welcome a few " superior " townspeople.
Doctors, attorneys, and—of course—clergymen, are
included, as well as officers, naval or military,
retired or on promotion. Elizabeth's " He is a
gentleman, I am a gentleman's daughter," defines the enclosure. The men, presumably, have
business to transact, affairs to arrange. They read
the newspapers and talk politics—among themselves. But Miss Austen does not concern herself with these aspects of life. Her heroines are
not so gay as Miss Burney's ; they are not so
thoroughly " in the swim." But her picture is
similarly one of home life, varied by " visiting "
and " receiving." She describes the distribution
of one family into several — by " suitable "
marriages. One section of English society, at one

period, in the home, is completely brought to life again.

Miss Brontë, even more thoroughly ignoring London, does not exhaustively represent any one class, and has, indeed, little concern with " manners." Nevertheless, practically all her characters have " something to do." They follow a profession, or own a factory. Clergymen are still largely in evidence, but education—in different forms—has come to the front, and, what is still more significant, some of her heroines have to work for their living. Wherefore, apart from the increased intensity of emotion, the external atmosphere is far more strenuous, and in Shirley we even find the dawn of a social problem, echoes of the early struggle between Capital and Labour. The pictures of school life, at home and abroad, do not merely reproduce facts, but cry out for improvements. The intimate knowledge of Continental conditions is, in itself, a new feature.

Finally, George Eliot extends the sphere of action in many directions. Maintaining the middle-class realism of Richardson, in her case largely concentrated on small-town tradesmen and farmers, she still avoids London, but embraces every " profession," and approaches, by expert study for " copy," the labourers and mechanics " discovered " by Victorian novelists. She travels lower and more widely than her predecessors for atmosphere. She does not confine herself, like them, to personal experience. In *Felix Holt* she deliberately arranges for the illustration of economic politics ; in *Daniel Deronda* she opens a big " race " problem ; in *Romola* she essays " historical " romance. The passionate emotional outbursts of Charlotte Brontë have become psychological analyses ; " problems " of all sorts are discussed with philosophical composure and professional knowledge. Within her self-imposed limits, woman has covered the field.

For the revelation of womanhood, through the types chosen for heroines, we find that Miss Burney still idealises a form of " sensibility," which does not exhibit much advance on the ethereal purity of the old-world romance. The difference, however, is important, since the type is studied from life, not created by the imagination. The essential features of this quality are susceptibility to the fine shades, delicate refinement, and an exalted ideal of love. It is itself thoroughly romantic, and separates heroines from ordinary mortals. Similar characteristics, if betrayed by men, may be attractive, but do not command respect.

Jane Austen, planting her challenge in the very title of her first novel, extols sense. Marianne, and—more subtly, perhaps—her mother, remain to secure our affection for a vanishing feminine grace ; but, evidently, the type cannot survive the century. For, though few writers have actually said less about the rights of women or the problems of sex, no one has established with more undaunted conviction the progress to a new position. Gaily, and with well-assumed irresponsibility, brushing aside for ever " the advantages of folly in a pretty girl," Jane *assumes*—with irresistible good humour — woman's intellectual equality in everything that really matters. Catherine Morland is obviously a relic, conceived of parody ; and Fanny Price was born at a disadvantage. Generally speaking, her heroines judge for themselves as a matter of course, and judge wisely. They even " judge for " the men. Their charm arises from mental independence.

Though to our modern notions their lives may

seem empty enough, a thousand and one touches
reveal advance on the eighteenth-century conception of " what is becoming to elegant females."
They demand rational occupation, common-sense
culture, the right to express themselves. They
fall in love at the dictate of their own hearts.
They set the standard of fidelity. It is true that
Colonel Brandon's adopted daughter and Maria
Bertram submit to convention, and that Lydia
Bennet is let off more easily because Darcy
had " patched up " the affair ; but the feeling
about purity is sound and clear—that is, feminine.
The " sense of sin " experienced by Jane Fairfax
may be a little strained, but we meet with no
high-flown notions of self-sacrifice in Emma ;
Elizabeth encourages Darcy to an explanation ;
and women are no longer afraid of happiness.
They have grown to recognise that their life is in
their own hands, not in those of man ; that it is
largely in their own power to shape their own
destiny ; that they will be wise to create their
own standard of conduct, to settle their own
affairs. The ideal emerging is startlingly modern
in essentials. Though the problems confront-
ing us to-day have not arisen, we feel that Jane

Austen's young ladies could have faced them
with equanimity, possibly with a more balanced
judgment than our own. There is a hint, indeed,
in *Mansfield Park* that the poor woman may one
day triumph over her sisters of leisure ; for are
not Fanny, William, and even Susan, the only
real " comforts " to their elders ? Sir Thomas
" saw repeated, and for ever repeated, reason
to . . . acknowledge the advantages of early
hardship and discipline and the consciousness of
being born to struggle and endure."

Curiously enough, Charlotte Brontë, while
uttering the first feminine protest, seems to have
slipped back somewhat on this question. Taking
for text Anne Elliot's claim that women love
longer without hope or life, she demands, even for
Shirley, a male " master." The explanation of this
attitude was partly temperament—since women of
vigorous intellect always need a flesh and blood
prophet (witness Harriet Martineau and George
Eliot) : and it arose partly from her individual
circumstances. The men of her family were, in
different ways, exasperatingly weak ; the " strong "
men of her native moorlands were naturally
domineering : her imagination was stirred, and her

mind trained, by the Belgian Professor, Monsieur Heger, who *was* her master—technically, and who —as we learn from independent testimony—always took a delight in scolding his pupils. We do not, to-day, admire the feminine footstool; nevertheless Charlotte Brontë's heroines have strong individual character, and are much given to defying the world. The type will never become popular in fiction, it is too angular intellectually, and too discontented. The quality of physical plainness has been seldom adopted by novelists, male or female. But in *Shirley* Miss Brontë generously abandons many of her favourite ideals, for *both* heroines. The types are mixed here; and we must feel that had circumstances encouraged a larger output, we might be compelled to modify many of our conclusions. It remains a fact that the authoress of *Jane Eyre* and *Villette* does not stand in the direct line of progress: save that she introduces the awakening of women to serious topics, and proves them intent not merely on self-revelation, but on reform. Her central inspiration, however, is passion: which no woman had hitherto handled; which few have since so powerfully portrayed.

It is not easy, even if possible, to summarise the more complex, and much varied, ideals of womanhood exhibited by George Eliot. Each of her heroines is a study from life ; and, by this time, women were not all created in one pattern. Again, we can scarcely say that she has given us a heroine in *Adam Bede*, whereas *Middlemarch* might claim to offer three. Maggie Tulliver shows little resemblance to Romola. Yet, undoubtedly, George Eliot had more conscious, and more definite, theories on women than any of her predecessors : she deliberately set out to expound and enforce them.

We are tempted, however, to conclude that her favourite ideal was self-sacrifice. Her outlook was inclined to be melancholy ; and she introduces us to that struggle between temperament and circumstances which is the keynote of modern fiction, forming the problem novel. In Fanny Burney and Jane Austen the heroine was simply more refined, or more sensible, than her family ; and the story was founded on this difference. In George Eliot each heroine has her own temperament and her own set of circumstances which create her own problem. Women are now no

longer concerned only with manners and delicacy :
they have entered into life as a whole. The
central fact, which may be seen in the earliest
women-writers, is now expressed and deliberately
put forward—that their moral standard is higher
than men's, that they have been treated unfairly
by the world. Charlotte Brontë had emphasised
this protest on one question, George Eliot applies
it everywhere.

The elementary truth which the women novelists revealed (and for which they were censured
by masculine critics) was that women do fall in
love without waiting to be wooed. George Eliot
develops this into a declaration of feminine judgment on life and character. Woman is no longer
man-made, man-taught, or man-led. The door is
opened for her independence.

Finally, it must not be forgotten that—whether
intentionally or by instinct concerned with the
revelation of their own nature—the great women-
writers have been always awake to the humour
of life. One says continually that women *have*
no sense of humour ; but this mistake arises from
generalisings, where the true test can only be
applied by discrimination. Nothing differs so

widely between *individuals* as the appreciation
of humour ; though it is true that much masculine
wit, tending towards farce, appeals to few
women.

In our " leading ladies " (here scarcely including
Charlotte Brontë) we find peculiar power and
extensive variety. Fanny Burney depends on
an eye for comedy, Jane Austen on the humorous
phrase, George Eliot on the study of wit.

In *Evelina* and *Cecilia* the comic effects are
mostly produced by the sudden meeting of
opposites ; the gay, irresponsible exaggeration
of types ; the clash of circumstances. Dickens,
consciously or unconsciously, borrowed much of
his method from Fanny Burney. The characters
of each have their allotted foible, their catch
phrase, their moral label, which somehow delights
and surprises us afresh, however expected, at
each repetition. Those inherently uncongenial
are forced into close contact, one exposing the
other. Speaking roughly, this is the stage manner.
Could we not fancy the speakers confronted, and
imagine their expressions of mutual astonishment,
there would be little fun in them. They are not
always quite so comic to our eyes as in each other's.

Captain Mirvan needs Madame Duval as a foil; that egregious fop Lovel is always playing up to Mrs. Selwyn; and, if Miss Branghton does not herself see the humour of the inimitable Smith, she brings it out. In *Cecilia*, again, the guardians produce each other; the "Larolles" is never so happy as when expounding Mr. Meadows; Mr. Gosport requires an audience.

Miss Burney's wit is the child of Society generated in a crowd; it savours of repartee. Although spontaneous and true to life, it does not flash out from the nature of things, but from deliberate arrangement. It has been sought and is found. The material is well chosen. The people are "put together" for our amusement.

Jane Austen has used, and refined, this method — as she has adapted everything from Miss Burney—in her earlier work. The titles—*Pride and Prejudice, Sense and Sensibility*—and the ideas behind them betray their own inspiration. Elizabeth Bennet, clearly, is *intended* to strike fire from Mr. Collins and Lady Catherine; Mrs. Bennet would scarcely have seemed so funny to another husband. The "Burney" innocence of Catherine Morland tempts Isabella to extremes in knowing vulgarity ; Mrs. Jennings cannot ruffle Lady Middleton.

But on her own account, and in her best moments, Miss Austen is far more subtle. Hers is an intimate humour, dependent on shades, not contrasts, of character. Even the more boisterous figures of fun, even Catherine's ridiculous applications of Udolpho, are complete in themselves, needing no foil. Miss Austen possesses a humorous imagination, where Miss Burney could only observe. A mere list of her quaint characters would fill a chapter, and no one of them is only comic. They are human beings, not mere puppets set up to laugh at. Moreover, the humour of them is derived from the polished phrase. Generally a few words suffice, fit though few.

Most assuredly, on the other hand, Miss Austen does not depend for her humour upon her comic characters. To begin with, these are never dragged in for " relief," they " belong to " the plot ; and in the second place, much of her most perfect satire arises from 'scenes in which they have no part. We have, for example, the dialogue on generosity between Mr. and Mrs. John Dashwood ; the paragraph about " natural folly in a beautiful

girl " ; Miss Bingley's ideal for a ball ; Harriet's
" most precious treasures " ; Sir Thomas Bertram's complacent pride in Fanny ; Mary Mus-
grave's anxiety about " the precedence that was
her due " ; with other incidents too numerous to
mention.

The fact is that almost every sentence of Miss
Austen's is pointed with humour ; the finished
phrasing of her narrative and her descriptions are
unrivalled in wit. There is no strain or distortion,
no laboured antithesis or uncouth dialect : merely
the light touch, the unerring instinct for the happy
phrase. At times we can detect indignation behind the laughter : her scorn is often most biting,
she indulges in cynicism. But, in the main, her
object is plainly derisive : the sheer joy of merri-
ment, the consolation of meeting folly with a gay
heart. And analysis will prove that, in her
opinion, hypocrisy and pose are the sins unfor-
givable, the only legitimate occasion of joy to the
jester. Elizabeth may turn off her discomfiture
with a joke, but in reality she is honest, and
wise enough to know that Darcy is unassailable
by reason of his good qualities.

The attributes Miss Austen ridicules are those

she seriously despises or dislikes, however gener
ously she often secures our affection for their
possessors. Her " figures of fun " are not wholly
despicable.

Attention has been drawn of late to a marked
contrast between the French comedy of " social
gesture "—which is entirely intellectual—and the
whole-souled laughter of the English. Shakespeare's comic " figures are not a criticism of
life—no great English literature is that. It is
a piece of life imaginatively realised. Falstaff is
not judged, he is accepted. Dogberry is not
offered as a fool to be ridiculed by his intellectual
betters. We are not asked to deride him. We
are asked to become part of his folly. Falstaff
appeals to the Falstaff in ourselves. Dogberry is
our common stupidity, enjoyed for the sake of the
dear fool that is part of every man. Shakespeare's
laugh includes vice and folly in a humour which
is the tolerance of Nature herself for all her works.'
. . . English laughter lives in good fellowship."

Since Macaulay did not hesitate to compare
Jane Austen with Shakespeare in one matter, we
may repeat his audacity here. The definition, if
definition it can be called, will surely apply to

Emma and *Pride and Prejudice*. They are "*pieces of life imaginatively realised.*" We laugh *with* the eccentricities, not *at* them. Properly speaking, Miss Austen is no satirist. She can amuse us without killing emotion.

As hinted already, Charlotte Brontë has neither humour nor wit. She takes life most seriously; and, in attempting a comic relief, becomes lumping or savage. The fact of her "Shirley" curates recognising, and enjoying, their own portraits may serve to measure the limit of her success. Such men could only enjoy the second-rate. Her satire against charity schools and Belgian pensionnats is mere spite.

We must pass on, therefore, to George Eliot, who certainly had wit, and was once acclaimed very humorous. Here, as elsewhere, our authoress appears to have gathered up the resources of her predecessors, developed them by study and culture, dressed them up in the language of the professional. The fact that the mechanism of her humour can be analysed, however, must prove its limitation. It is "worked in," skilfully, but obviously. There is everywhere an "impression of highly-wrought sentences which are meant to arrest the reader's attention and *warn him what he is to look for* of tragedy, of humour, of philosophy." The humour is obviously " composed " to heighten the tragic effect by contrast.   In her earlier work, indeed, every form of elaboration in style was but " one sign of her overmastering emotion," therefore " fitting and suitable " ; but repetition made it tedious and mechanical. After a time we see through " the expression of a humorous fancy in a pedantic phrase ; the reminiscence of a classical idiom applied to some everyday triviality ; the slight exaggeration of verbiage which is to accentuate an aphorism . . moulded on the plaster casts of the schools."

The fact is that humour, and even wit, flourish most happily in uncultured fields—for there is only one George Meredith.   Yet, within her limitations, there is triumph for the genius of George Eliot. None can deny tribute to Mrs. Poyser, or the " Aunts " in *The Mill on the Floss*. That very severe study and applied observation, which kills spontaneity, lent her the power to excite tears and laughter. She has given us oddities as rugged as, and more various than, Miss Burney's, contrasts of manners as bustling ; scenes

and persons as humanly humorous as Jane
Austen's.   She combines their methods, enrich-
ing them by dialect, antithesis, allusion, and the
" study " of types.   There is humour *and* wit in
her work.

If, as we certainly admit, both are " worked
out " carefully and the labour shows through,
we must also acknowledge that she has embraced,
and extended, all the achievements of woman
before her day, indicating the powers realised and
the possibilities to be accomplished

THE WOMAN'S MAN

ALTHOUGH, as we have seen everywhere, the
women novelists did so much in lifting the veil
and, so to speak, giving themselves away; they
also held up the mirror to man's complacency,
and, in a measure, enabled the other sex to see
himself as they saw him. In the process they
created a type, beloved of schoolgirls, which can
only be described as the "Woman's Man," and
must be admitted a partial travesty on human
nature. It does not, however, reveal any less
insight than much of man's feminine portraiture.

Curiously enough, the earliest "Woman's Man"
in fiction was of male origin. We all know how
Richardson, having given us Clarissa, was invited
to exert his genius upon the "perfect gentleman."
But the little printer had ever an eye on the ladies,
and, whether or no of malice prepense, drew the
immaculate Sir Charles Grandison—frankly, in
every particular—not as he must have known him
in real life, but rather according to the pretty

fancy of the dear creatures whose entreaties
had called into being the gallant hero.

And, as elsewhere, Fanny Burney took up the
type, refined it, and lent an attractive subtlety
to that somewhat monumental erection of the
infallible. The actual imaginings of woman are
proved less wooden than Richardson supposed
them, and infinitely more like human nature.
In many things Lord Orville resembles Sir Charles.
He is scarcely less perfect, but his empire is more
restricted. The chorus of admiration granted to
Grandison, and his astounding complacency, are
replaced by the unconscious revelations of innocent
girlhood naturally expressing her simple enthusiasm
to the kindest of foster-parents. The peerless
Orville, indeed, is not exactly a " popular " hero.
It needs a superior mind to appreciate his
superiority ; and we suspect there were circles
in which he was voted a " prodigious dull fellow."
His life was not passed in an atmosphere of worship. It is only in the heart of Evelina that he
is king. Nor can we fancy Miss Burney submitting
her heroine to the ignominy, as modern readers
must judge it, of patiently and contentedly waiting, like Harriet Byron, until such time as his

majesty should determine between the well-
balanced claims of herself and her rival to the
honour of his hand. Personally, we have never
been able to satisfy ourselves whether Grandison
loved Clementina more or less than Harriet ; if
he was properly " in love " with either.

It was, indeed, rather becoming so fine a
gentleman to be wooed than to woo ; and
the visit to Italy was, in all likelihood, actually
brought in as an afterthought, mainly designed to
illustrate the power of conscience over a good
man. Anyone less perfect than Sir Charles would
be universally charged with having compromised
Clementina ; and the real motive of his English
"selection in wives" was to escape the consequences
of an entanglement involving difficulties about
religion and constant association with the Italian
temperament. Having thoroughly investigated the
circumstances and judicially examined his own
heart, the cool-headed young man decides that he
is not in honour bound ; gently but firmly severs
the somewhat embarrassing connection ; and, in
dignified language, communicates his decision to
" the other lady." Humbly and gratefully she
accepts his self-justification and his love. It is

obvious that no one could ever have either refused him or questioned the dictates of his conscience. But as Jane Austen remarks, in a very different connection, " It is a new circumstance in romance, I acknowledge, and dreadfully derogatory of a heroine's dignity." No woman writer would permit it.

Nevertheless, in the essential qualities of heart and mind, no less than in the heroine's mental attitude towards their perfections, Lord Orville and Sir Charles Grandison belong to the same order of men : made by women for women. So far as I am aware, Miss Burney originated the semi-paternal relationship (reappearing, with variations, in Knightley and Henry Tilney) which certainly helped to deceive Evelina as to the state of her heart, and has in itself a peculiar charm. There is real delicacy, quite beyond Richardson or his Sir Charles, in Orville's repeated attempts to preserve Evelina from her own ignorance ; to give her (as none of her natural guardians ever attempted) some slight knowledge of the world ; protect her from insult ; and advise her in diffi culty. He never intrudes or presumes ; and, because, after all, women's first and last mission as novel-writers was the refinement of fiction, it cannot be too often emphasised that Miss Burney was most extraordinarily refined for her age. The very coarseness in certain externals which she admits without protest, should serve only to establish her own innate superiority.

But it remains true that the essential attribute of Orville, as of Grandison, was perfectibility. He is a very Bayard, the *preux chevalier*, and the Sir Galahad of eighteenth-century drawing-rooms. Neither the author, nor her heroine, would have ever imagined it possible to criticise this prince of gentlemen. It really pained them when persons of inferior breeding or less exalted morality occasionally ventured to oppose his will or question his judgment. His praise, and his love, were alike a mighty condescension ; his mere notice an honour almost greater than they could bear.

This is the modern, civilised notion of knighthood ; the personification (in terms of everyday life) of that pure dream which has haunted, and will ever haunt, the musings of maidenhood ; the pretty fancy that one day He, prince of fairyland, will ride into her very ordinary little existence, acclaim her queen, and carry her away somewhere to be happy ever after. Miss Burney translated the vision for her generation, making it, verily, not greatly dissimilar from actual human experience.

We shall see later how certain women of the Victorian era visualised the same ideal.

In the numberless remarkable signs of feminine advance between the authoress of *Evelina* and Jane Austen we find that this particular attitude and ideal has almost completely vanished. The hero is no longer quite perfect; condescension is not now his most conspicuous virtue. The heroine, indeed, has become the one woman who ventures to criticise him. Darcy learns quite as much from Elizabeth as she from him. As already hinted, " Mr. Knightley " is the nearest approach in Jane Austen to the old type. He is the only person in Highbury who " ventured to criticise Emma "—without being sufficiently snubbed for his pains. He is, admittedly, the personification of superiority; though he is not very " sure of the lady." Again the character is gently satirised in Henry Tilney, the situation of Northanger Abbey, as we have said above, being a more subtle parody of Evelina than of Udolpho. The young clergyman is nearly faultless. Catherine swears by him in everything—from theology to "sprigged muslin." He, too, teaches her all she ever knew about the "great world"; and guides her, without a rival in authority, among the bewildering intricacies of men and books.

But, in her own domain and as to her most original creations, Miss Austen has been criticised for her occasional lack of insight towards men. It may be true, indeed, that neither Darcy nor Knightley always speaks, or behaves, quite like a gentlemen; which means that, like all women, she had not an absolutely unerring instinct for the things which are "not done." In all probability, as men will never quite understand women's emotional purity, women will never fully appreciate men's alert sense of honour. Generally speaking, of course, the feminine standard in all things is far higher than the masculine; and the women novelists have done much in pulling us up to their level. But there are a few points, which concern deeper issues than social polish, of which few women, if any, can attain to the absolute ideal of chivalry.

There are, of course, many more superficial aspects by which the men in Jane Austen may be easily recognised as woman-made. We hear com-

paratively little of their point of view in affairs of
the heart, with which the novels are mainly concerned, save in that most thoughtful passage
closing *Persuasion* ; and we know even less of their
attitude towards ethics, citizenship. business, or
social problems. Only clergymen or sailors are
shown to be even superficially concerned with any
profession in life ; and this is merely because the
authoress was personally intimate with both. It
is, in fact, an infallible instinct for her own limitations which saved her from more obvious failure
as a portrait-painter of men. Man at the tea-
table is her chosen theme ; and this too is a work
which could not have been safely entrusted to any
male pen.

The Brontës, on the other hand, exhibit a
startlingly original and unexpected revival of the
early type, in the central feature of its conception.
Here once more the hero is most emphatically
" the master "—of body and soul. Jane Eyre, we
remember, loved—and served—her " employer " ;
Lucy Snowe and Shirley their " teachers." There
are, probably, no more arrogant males in fiction
than these gentlemen ; no more enslaved female
worshippers. Yet the combination is totally un-

like the Richardson-Burney brand. To begin with,
the dominant, and domineering, hero is represented
in each case as almost, if not quite, unique ; not as
the man normal. Nor are we called upon to admire
without qualification. There is nothing ideal about
Rochester, Monsieur Heger, Paul Emmanuel, or
Louis Moore. The Brontë heroines did not at all
admire perfection in man, and they abominated
good looks. Nor were they, on the other hand,
in the least humble by nature, generally yielding
and clinging, or ever gateful for guidance and
information. They had no patience and very
little respect for the genus Homo.

There is, indeed, a touch of melodrama in the
sharp contrast exhibited between their proud
prickliness towards mankind and their idolatry of
The Man. Few women have written more bitterly
of our idle vanity, our heartless neglect and supreme
selfishness, our blind folly, and our indifference to
moral standards. None has spoken with more
biting emphasis of woman's natural superiority,
or of the grinding tyranny which, for so many
generations, she is herein shown to have stupidly
endured. Yet Charlotte Brontë has declared, without qualification and more frankly than any of

her sisters, that no woman can really love a man incapable of mastery ; that she is ever longing for the whip.

To assert herself, to demand liberty or even equality, is uncongenial ; and the aggressive attitude is only adopted as a duty, undertaken for the weaker sister from a passionate instinct for justice and an intolerance of sham. There were two things Charlotte Brontë hated : a handsome man and a deceitful woman. But hate left her very weary. It was the strain of playing prophetess that inspired her taste for " doormats."

Obviously, the conception of a Hero thus evolved is essentially feminine. The most complacently conservative among us, however intolerant of the fine shades, could never have either conceived or admired a Rochester. We should certainly not suppose him attractive to any woman of character. To us he appears mere tinsel, the obvious counterfeit and exaggeration of a type we have come to despise a little at its best. Naturally, such men fancy that they can " do what they like with the women " ; but *we* knew better, until the novelist confirmed the truth of their boast. Miss Brontë, moreover, is very much farther from our idea of a gentleman than Miss Austen. It may be doubted if men ever like or applaud rudeness, which she apparently considers essential to honest manliness.

Yet, however unique in its external manifestations, and however exaggerated in expression, the Brontë hero - recipe involves, like Miss Burney's, an assumption that happy marriages are achieved by meeting mastery with submission. However diverse their conceptions of the proper everyday balance between the sexes, both find their *ideal* in the absolute monarchy of Man.

It must be always more difficult and more hazardous to determine an author's private point of view as her art becomes more professional and self-conscious. George Eliot's characters are all deliberate studies, neither the instinctive expression of an ideal nor the unconscious reflection of experience ; and such manufactured products naturally tend to be extensively varied, seeking to avoid repetition or even similarity. We may, perhaps, say that George Eliot, out of her wider experience and more scholarly training, understood men better than her predecessors. She certainly avoided, as did Jane Austen, the specific " Woman's Man " ; and, on the other hand, she penetrated, without losing her way, more deeply into the masculine mystery than the creator of Messrs. Elton and Collins.

Tom Tulliver's whole relationship with his sister is an admirable study in the conventional notion of a stupid man's " superiority " to a clever woman ; but it cannot be criticised, or in any way regarded, as a feminine conception. That provokingly worthy and obstinate young man is perfectly true to life. There is neither mistake nor exaggeration here. We must all feel that " this lady " knows. In marriage, Tom would certainly have played the master to any woman " worthy of him," but would not thereby have become less normal or natural. If men question or puzzle over anything in *The Mill on the Floss*, it is not Maggie's toleration of Tom, but her temporary infatuation for Stephen. He indeed is something of a lady's man, not a woman's ; but probably we may not disown the type. To some extent, again, Adam Bede is " masterly " to his mother, and would probably---barring accidents on which the plot hinges—have been accepted by Hetty in the same spirit ; but he is certainly *not* perfect, and seldom, if ever, outruns probability.

But although George Eliot, having a wide out-look, recognises and illustrates the tendency in man to play the master, she does not associate it with any idea of perfection, nor does she idealise submission in women. Yet we know that personally, though less intensely than Charlotte Brontë, she too disliked sex-assertion, and found comfort in what the other only desired, a large measure of intellectual rest, by letting a man think and act for her. At all times her religion and her philosophy were largely borrowed or reflective—for all their assumption of independence—and every page of her life reveals the carefully protective influence of George Henry Lewes. Only less than any of the other chief women novelists did George Eliot permit self-expression in her work, and the particular portraiture of man we are here discussing was not the result of study but the exposure of conviction.

Finally, it was reserved for later writers, not of supreme genius, to develop the type to its extremity. Charlotte Yonge, with her usual superabundance of dramatis personæ, has *two* " women's men " in *The Heir of Redclyffe*, and the contrast between them is most instructive. The aggressive " perfection " of Philip, indeed, is crude enough. Miss Yonge deliberately exaggerates his manifold virtues in order to darken the evil within. The reader and

his own conscience alone ever realise the full force
of his jealous suspicions and obstinacy in self-justification. Guy's faults, on the other hand, are all
on the surface ; but his exalted saintliness is even
more superhuman than the other's unerring morality.
Both exemplify a feminine ideal ; though Philip
has only one worshipper, her faith is unfaltering.
His, indeed, is the type that lives to hold forth, to
inform, and to dogmatise. Woe to the woman
who ventures to think for herself. The power or
charm of Guy is unconscious. They love his passionate outbursts, his generous impetuosity, his childish
remorse and " sensibility."   In him, however, there
are *some* qualities which men esteem : he was a
sportsman, adventurous, and transparently sincere.
Only his final " conversion " and the death-bed
scene spoil the picture. He becomes, in the end
(what Philip had always been), the sport of feminine
imagination with its craving for perfectibility. He
loses the human touch, vanishing among the gods.

We have the " last word " in this matter
from *John Halifax, Gentleman*. With schoolgirl
naïveté Phineas tells us on every page that " there
was never any man like him." His smile, his tenderness, his courage, his independence, his tact and

tyranny in the home, his quiet influence on Capital and Labour, are certainly unique, and no less certainly monotonous. He *understands* everybody, and " deals with them " easily. It costs him nothing to lead men and dominate women. Quietly and without effort, he pursues his way—to an admiring chorus, always " the master," the perfect gentleman. He was dignified, attractive, and very " particular over his daintiest of cambric and finest of lawn." The little waif of the opening chapters indignantly repudiated the name of " beggar-boy " : " You mistake ; I never begged in my life : I am a person of independent property, which consists of my head and my two hands, out of which I hope to realise a large capital some day." And he kept his word.

Prompt and acute in business, of unflinching integrity, and guided by generous understanding as to the serious labour problems of his generation, John was one of those fine English tradesmen who effected so much, not only towards the foundation of our commercial empire, but towards removing the barriers between their own class and a Society largely composed of " fox-hunting, drinking, dicing fools." The girl who loved him was " shocked " to hear of his being " in business," although her feelings quickly developed to proud worship.

It is here, indeed, that Mrs. Craik reveals most power. Towards the " world "—his equals, his " men," or his " superiors "—John Halifax is the true gentleman, and a splendid specimen of manhood. He has rare dignity, shrewd insight, and ready command of language. The scene of his " drawing-room " fracas with Richard Brithwood is extremely dramatic, and gives us almost a higher opinion of the hero than any other. Entirely free from the narrow-mindedness of the ordinary self-made man, he almost subdues our dislike of the gentle despotism which he assumes towards wife and family. The complacent masculinity is exaggerated by the author's persistence in keeping him to the centre of the picture ; and we are disposed to believe that it might have been less open to criticism if expressed, as well as conceived, by a woman. Phineas Fletcher, the fictional Ego, has some charm ; but he is absolutely feminine, if not womanish, and the Jonathan-David attitude of every page becomes wearisome by repetition. There is no doubt that this perpetual enthusiasm of one man for another offends our taste, and has a tendency to make both a little ridiculous. John has a positive weakness for perfection, and we should observe the fact with more pleasure if it were less frequently " explained."

Here the man creates his surroundings or sets the tone, presumably exemplifying the author's ideal. He is singularly pure-minded, preposterously domestic, and very confident about the natural supremacy of man. It is the immense amount of tender detail, the infinite number of soft touches which convict the author of femininity. Her hero, however, is no knight of romance, no Bayard of the drawing-room, no love-lorn youth of dreams, no " fine gentleman," the mate of a girl's sensibility. He is not all soul and heart. He is of tougher fibre in groundwork (despite his " halo "), and primarily practical. Concerned externally with such tough problems as trade depression, the " bread riots," and the introduction of machinery, he is more often placed before us as lover, husband, father, and friend. Frank and decisive, he has remarkable self-control, and remains ideally simple. He has no doubts about sin and goodness, indifference or faith. We should be tempted to say that he spent his life in the nursery, though sometimes, indeed, the view of the nursery is not unworthy of our attention :

" I delighted to see dancing. Dancing, such as it was then, when young people moved breezily and lightly, as if they loved it ; skimming like swallows down the long line of the Triumph—gracefully winding in and out through the graceful country-dance—lively always, but always decorous. In those days people did not think it necessary to the pleasures of dancing that any stranger should have the liberty to snatch a shy, innocent girl round the waist, and whirl her about in mad waltz or awkward polka, till she stops, giddy and breathless, with burning cheek and tossed hair, looking— as I would not have liked to see our pretty Maud look."

Most of us, I fancy, would think better of John without Phineas at his elbow, if he were less supremely self-conscious, less given to that analysis of his own acts and emotions which is essentially feminine. But Mrs. Craik will not let her hero alone. She thrusts him upon us without mercy, till we are driven to cry " halt." We are convinced that no human being could comfortably carry about with him so heavy a burden of perfectibility. He is (as women have often fancied us) not what we are but what she would have us be ; and here, as elsewhere, even the Ideal does not please man.

PERSONALITIES

ALL art is the expression of an individuality, and
environment has some influence on genius. Without question *Evelina* and *Cecilia* owe much to
the accidents of Miss Burney's own experience.
Hers, indeed, was an eventful, almost romantic,
life. To-day we only remember Dr. Burney as
the father of Fanny ; but he was a man of mark
in his own generation, and his industrious enthusiasm was obviously infectious. Fanny was
not early distinguished among his clever children,
and we must conclude that she had something of
that delicate refinement granted her heroines,
making her rather shy and diffident among the
mixed gatherings in which he took such pride
and delight. As one of her sisters remarked, this
lack of self-confidence gave her at times the appearance of hauteur ; and it is quite obvious that
no suspicions could have been aroused in any of
them of her capacity for " taking notes." Hers
was always the quiet corner where " the old
lady," as they called her at home, could observe

the quality, occasionally join in a spirited conversation, and—after her own fashion—enjoy " the
diversions." Her characteristics, says fourteen-
year-old Susan, " seem to be sense, sensibility,
and bashfulness, even to prudery." It would be
kinder, perhaps, to credit her with modesty such
as we find expressed in her own account of *Evelina ;
or, A Young Lady's Entrance into the World* :

" Perhaps this may seem rather a bold attempt
and title for a female whose knowledge of the world
is very confined, and whose inclinations, as well as
situation, incline her to a private and domestic life.
All I can urge is, that I have only presumed to trace
the accidents and adventures to which a ' young woman '
is liable ; I have not pretended to shew the world
what it actually *is*, but what it *appears* to a young
girl of seventeen : and so far as that, surely any girl
who is past seventeen may safely do ? The motto
of my excuse shall be taken from Pope's *Temple of
Fame* :

  ' In every work, regard the author's end ;
   None e'er can compass more than they intend.' "

How far she had actually experienced adventures,
or at least met characters, similar to those of her
novel, her entertaining Diaries most abundantly
illustrate. One is almost ashamed before the
enthusiasm which, between domesticities con-

sidered becoming a lady, secretarial work for Dr.
Burney, and voluminous letters to her faithful
friend Daddy Crisp, the authoress accomplished
so much in so comparatively short a period.

For she had not only to " scribble " *Evelina*, but
to copy it all out in a feigned upright hand.   It was
natural enough that Lowndes, bookseller, should
have refused to publish without the whole manuscript, but equally natural that she should complain :

" This man, knowing nothing of my situation, sup
posed, in all probability, that I could sit quietly at my
bureau, and write on with expedition and ease, till the
work was finished.   But so different was the case, that
I had hardly time to write half a page a day ; and
neither my health nor inclination would allow me to
continue my *nocturnal* scribbling for so long a time, as
to write first, and then copy, a whole volume.   I was
therefore obliged to give the attempt and affair entirely
over for the present."

Genius, of course, would not be stifled ; and, in
the end, she completed her work within the year,
gaily accepting the payment of £20 down for the
copyright, to which the publisher added £10 when
its success was assured by a sale of 2300 copies
during 1778.

Frances Burney became immediately the pet of

Society. The diaries of this period are crowded with records of flattery which may seem extravagant, if not ludicrous, to modern reticence ; and she has been criticised for repeating them. Yet for us it is fortunate that there were " two or three persons," for whom her diaries were written, " to whom her fame gave the purest and most exquisite delight." They have become history, and, as Macaulay remarks, " nothing can be more unjust than to confound these outpourings of a kind heart, sure of perfect sympathy, with the egotism of a blue-stocking who prates to all who come near her about her own novel or her own volume of sonnets."

The fact is that, by a comparison with the Early Diaries, we may feel confident that Miss Burney was never spoilt by popularity. Inevitably she came out of the shade, talked more as she was more often singled out for compliments or conversation ; but there is no appearance of conceit, and little increase in self-confidence. The youthful simplicity of her work remains her prevailing characteristic ; and the slight maturity of *Cecilia*, not always an advantage, is obviously no more than a desire to please. It is not her own sense of dignity in authorship, but the pride of Crisp and the affection

of Dr. Johnson which stimulates the effort. Always
" instinct with the proprieties and the delicacies
implanted by careful guardians,"[1] it was her
business to " describe the world as it seems to a
woman utterly preoccupied with the thought of how
she seems to the world," to picture man " simply
and solely as a member of a family." One recognises the limit and single-mindedness of her aim,
in her reason for abandoning drama. She found she
could not " preserve spirit and salt, and yet keep
up delicacy."

We are all familiar enough to-day with the cruelty
of the reward by which foolish persons thought to
acknowledge her prowess. The five years' imprisonment at Court, though it could not ultimately
tame her spirit, brought about temporary physical
wreck, and seems to have lulled for ever the desire
for literary fame. We have endeavoured to show,
in an earlier chapter, that *Camilla* is not entirely
without significance ; but there can be no question
that after her marriage she wrote only for money,
and, if not without individuality, yet, as it were,
to order and by rule.

We are concerned here only with her earlier

[1] Her stepmother.

years, when she was the replica of her own heroines.

The real character of Miss Austen almost defies analysis. Contemporary evidence, of any discrimination, is practically non-existent; her life presents no outstanding adventure; and it is very dangerous to assume identity between any expression in the novels and her experience or opinion. As a matter of fact, she never even states a truth, exhibits an emotion, or judges a case except by implication. Even the apparent generalisations or author's comments on life are really attuned to the atmosphere of the particular novel in which they appear.

"It is a truth universally acknowledged," we read, "that a single man in possession of a good fortune must be in want of a wife." Miss Austen knows better. She is perfectly aware of the perverseness often exhibited by wealthy bachelors. The sentence is no more than a most ingenious stroke of art. It plunges us at once into the atmosphere of Meryton and the subject of the tale. It betrays Mrs. Bennet and, in a lesser degree, Lady Lucas. It prepares us for her vulgarity, at once distressing, and elevating by contrast, the refinement of Jane and Elizabeth. Never surely did a novel open with a paragraph so suggestive. Again, the first page of *Mansfield Park* contains a phrase of similar significance. The author remarks : " There certainly are not so many men of large fortune in the world as there are pretty women to deserve them." Again, she is not speaking in her own person. Lady Bertram felt this— so far as she ever formed an opinion for herself. Mrs. Norris and Mrs. Price had personal experience of its truth. The subtle irony reveals *their* point of view, not Miss Austen's.

It requires, of course, no particular subtlety to trace from her novels the type of character she approves and loves best, her general standard of manners and conduct, and her scorn for hypocrisy. We have even hazarded to affirm evidence for her opinions on one or two questions of more importance. But they do *not* reveal her personality in detail ; and to say, with her nephew, that she possessed all the charms of all her heroines, would be to make her inhuman.

There is, in fact, an undiscriminating conventionality about such descriptions as we possess which gives us no real information. We are told, for example, that

" her carriage and deportment were quiet, yet graceful. Her features were separately good. Their assemblage produced an unrivalled expression of that cheerfulness, sensibility, and benevolence which were her real characteristics. Her complexion was of the finest texture. It might with truth be said that her eloquent blood spoke through her modest cheek. Her voice was extremely sweet. She delivered herself with fluency and precision. Indeed, she was formed for elegant and rational society, excelling in conversation as much as in composition. In the present age it is hazardous to mention accomplishments. Our authoress would, probably, have been inferior to few in such acquirements had she not been so superior to most in higher things."

It would seem as if the writer were really intent on describing perfection.

And *yet*, we are convinced personally that Miss Austen had a peculiar charm of her own. Undoubtedly she lived among persons as empty-headed as those she has immortalised ; probably she had met Mrs. Norris, Mr. Elton, and Mr. Collins : apparently she was happy. No doubt her devotion to Cassandra (suggesting her partiality for sister-heroines) counted for much ; and all her family were agreeable. They had a good deal of " sense." Her life provided even less variety of incident than she discovered at Longbourn or

Uppercross ; and, if she was fond of reading, she knew nothing about literature. Her letters do not suggest the uneasiness attached to the possession of a soul—as we moderns understand it.

Yet one point merits attention and may partially reveal. There can be no question that the very breath of her art is satire, and she is at times even cynical. Yet the one thing we know positively of her private life is that she was a favourite aunt, a devoted sister, a sympathetic daughter. Now the child-lover, beloved of children, must possess certain qualities, which prove that her cynicism was not ingrained, misanthropic, or pessimistic ; that her pleasure in fun was neither ill-natured nor unsympathetic. There must have been strength of character in two directions not often united. Her life was, in a measure, isolated—from superiority. She gave more than she received. Nor can we believe her entirely unaware of what life might have yielded her in more equal companionship ; entirely without bitterness—for example—in the invention of Mrs. Norris. There can be no question, we think, that life never awakened the real Jane Austen. She lived absolutely in, and for, her art, of which the delight to her was supreme. Yet family tradition declares, with obvious truth, that her genius never tempted her to arrogance, affectation, or selfishness. She worked in the family sitting-room, writing on slips of paper that could immediately, without bustle or parade, be slipped *inside* her desk at the call of friendship or courtesy. At any moment she suffered interruption without protest. The absolute self-command so obvious in the work governed her life.

But we have always believed that one passage in *Pride and Prejudice* does give us a suggestive glimpse—again only by implication—of very real autobiography :

" ' You are a great deal too apt,' says Eliza to Jane Bennet, ' to like people in general. You never see a fault in anybody. All the world are good and agreeable in your eyes. I never heard you speak ill of a human being in my life.'

" ' I would not wish to be hasty in censuring anyone,' answers Jane, ' but I always speak what I think.'

" ' I know you do, and it is *that* which makes the wonder. With *your* good sense, to be so honestly blind to the follies and nonsense of others. Affectation of candour is common enough—one meets it everywhere. But to be candid without ostentation or design—to take the good of everybody's character and make it still better, and say nothing of the bad—belongs to you alone ' "

This is, we like to fancy, a portrait of her own sister, Cassandra. Jane Austen herself was *not* " a great deal too apt to like people in general," though she too could be marvellously tender with Marianne Dashwood, most " silly " of heroines, and her still more ridiculous mother. It is certain, indeed, that she never neglected even the most tiresome " neighbours," but she did not love them. There is evidence enough in *Persuasion* that she could sympathise with deep feelings, which were necessarily suppressed in such surroundings as she gives all her heroines, and had experienced herself.

Her reverend father, " the handsome proctor," like most clergymen of his generation, was essentially a country gentleman, not very much better educated, and scarcely more strenuous, than his neighbours. His wife took a simple and honest pride in the management of her household ; and his sons followed their father's footsteps, entered the navy, or pursued whatever other profession they could most *conveniently* enter. The whole atmosphere of the vicarage was complacently material and old-fashioned, where the ideas of progress filtered slowly and discontent was far from being considered divine. The personal aloofness from characters delineated, so conspicuous in her art, was borrowed from life. Everywhere, and always, the real Jane stood aside.

Nor were there granted her any of the consolations of culture. We have no doubt that she received no more education than might be acquired at Mrs. Goodard's :

" A school, not a seminary, or an establishment, or anything which professed, in long sentences of refined nonsense, to combine liberal acquirements with elegant morality, upon new principles and new systems—and when young ladies, for enormous pay, might be screwed out of health and into vanity—but a real, honest, old-fashioned boarding-school, where a reasonable quantity of accomplishments were sold at a reasonable price, and where girls might be sent out of the way and scramble themselves into a little education, without any danger of coming back prodigies."

It needed, perhaps, some such unromantic, unruffled, and unvaried existence, with a mind perfectly composed, to produce those six flawless works of art which remain for us the most complete expression of good sense, the most complete triumph over the fanciful exaggerations of romance. Genius alone could adjust the balance with such nicety and leave us content. She forces us, by sheer wit and sympathy, to love and admire the very persons of all time and place who have in themselves least to interest or attract.

The character of Charlotte Brontë, like her work, brings us at once into a new atmosphere. All here is emotionally strenuous, if not melodramatic. The bleak parsonage, the stern widowed father, the vicious son, the three wonderful sisters : around and about them the mysteries of *Wuthering Heights*. The picture of those lonely girls, all the world to each other and nothing to the world, dreaming and scribbling in the cold, without sympathy and without guidance, is stamped for ever on our imagination. We know something, moreover, from *Jane Eyre*, about their cruel experience of schooldays, something, from *Agnes Grey*, about their noble efforts at independence. Finally, we have studied and talked over " the Secret "—supposed to reconcile work and life. As to the main outlines of temperament, at any rate, there can be no question.

Charlotte Brontë's experience of life was strictly limited : she had little interest about the trivialities of the tea-table. But she observed keenly, had a tenacious memory, and felt with intensity.

Without hardness or conceit, she was entirely
self-centred : there is no aloofness about her
work : it centres passionately around the heroine,
reflecting her own emotional outlook. She took
life seriously, like her heroines : acutely sensitive
to words and looks ; caring nothing for what did
not personally affect her. No doubt there is
something Irish, something too of the grim moorlands, in that mysterious instinct which fired
Charlotte, and her sisters, to their perpetual ques-
tionings of Providence, their burning protests
against the harshness and hypocrisy of the world.
Circumstances stifle them and they must speak.
Speaking, they must strike.

Charlotte Brontë, indeed, lived almost as much
aside from the world as Jane Austen. But
Haworth was not Stevenage : the Rev. Patrick
was certainly not a " handsome proctor," and
Bramwell could never have risen in " the Service."
It was in nature, however, that the contrast is
most marked. The author of *Jane Eyre*, however
shy and unsociable, was not content to stand
aloof and look on. With little enough experience
of actualities, she was for ever *making life* for
herself, sending that plain, visionary, eager, and

sensitive ego of hers out into the world ; and uttering with fiery eloquence her comments on what
she imagined herself to have done and seen.
Until recently, indeed, we have supposed that even
the heart of her work, that passionate devotion
which she was the first of women to reveal, was
entirely imaginative, an *invention* created without
guidance from personal experience. Now evidence
has been published which scarcely permits doubt ;
that whereas, obviously, her pupil-teacherdom at
Brussels widened her social outlook, it also awoke
her heart. Charlotte Brontë, evidently, fell in love
with the "Professor" at the Pensionnat Heger ;
and thus gained the memory of passion. But it
may be reasonably questioned, after all, whether
the experience did much for her art. Since
Monsieur Heger, no less certainly, did not return
her love, and seldom even answered her letters,
he could not have taught her the mysteries ; and
as, like her heroines, she was fatally addicted to
exaggeration—in love or hate—it is not probable
that her heroes—or ideal men—bear any very
real likeness to him in character. After all, she
practically "invented" him, as independent
witnesses have established ; and the accident

of her idealisations centring about a living man is not particularly significant. Her attitude, and that of her heroines, towards mankind in general, and towards " the man " in particular, is really woven out of a strong imagination : and the essence of her being remains a dreamer's. *Jane Eyre* and *Villette* are, transparently, the work of one who created her own world for herself only ; and we need not modify this impression from any letters of hers ever printed or written. Emotionally she was nourished on her own thoughts ; and, in her case, we may read them fearlessly in her work. It was not her nature to suppress, or conceal, anything. *She has put herself on record.* Here lies the essential difference between her work and Miss Burney's or Jane Austen's. While they reflected, with almost unruffled enjoyment, the surface of life, she tore off the wrappings and revealed a Soul. That, too, was of her very self. She had missed everything that mattered. It was at once her consolation and her revenge to project herself into the heart of life, and tell the tale.

The character and experience of George Eliot is far more complex, like her achievement, than

that of those who preceded her. Like them,
bred in retirement, though among more strenuous
surroundings, her youth gave her also much insight into what life means to "small" people.
But there was a strong religious atmosphere around
her, accident gave her the early control of affairs,
and her education—of a later date—was more
thorough. Then came the stirring of doubt, from
associations with sceptics ; the professional training
from practical journalism ; and the "problem"
evoked by her friendship with George Henry
Lewes. Life was training her for modern work.

The intense seriousness, the active conscience
of primitive faith, remained always with her,
influencing characterisation. But it was the wider
teachings of philosophy, the later experiences, and
the conscious desire after advance that made her
didactic. Her letters reveal an unexpected
sentimentalism and an intense craving for personal
affection ; her teachings are all interpreted by
what she has read, or inspired by men she has
met ; but they are in touch with real life and
directed by real thought. It was her personal
experience and character which enabled George
Eliot to combine the "manners" comedy of

Fanny Burney and Jane Austen with Miss
Brontë's moral campaign ; to weld the message
of woman into modernity.

She was, however, before all things, a professional student of humanity.   Though she
actually commenced novelist at a comparatively
advanced age, the previous years, and every item
of character, had been a training for this work.
She observed with accuracy, remembered without
effort, and studiously cultivated her natural
literary powers.   Emotionally and intellectually she
got the most out of life ; never, perhaps, quite letting
herself go, but keenly alive to every impression, on
the alert for experience and information.   It was
not in her ever to let things alone.

Such a temperament, of course, does not produce either spontaneous fun, sleepless humour,
or unbridled self-torment ; but it acquires the
power of responding to all human difficulties,
understanding the " problem " of life, and sym-
pathising in its beauty and joy. George Eliot
was always pondering about truth, considering
the remedies for evil, looking forward towards
progress. Her own experience was utilised freely,
with an instinct for dramatic effect, but it is not

the whole body of her work. That was a deliberately composed art, put out as an instrument for a given purpose, studied and ornamented. But while thus nurtured and apart, it is also the expression of herself, the sum of her being. Therein, like an actress, she plays many parts, putting on the mood of each new story and living in it.

She is, in fact, a typical woman of letters, as we now understand the term, with all the excellences and all the limitations of even the greatest among us.

CONCLUSION

WE find, in the main, that women developed—and perfected—the domestic novel. They made circulating libraries respectable, establishing the right, and the power, of women to write fiction.

They carried on the traditions of Richardson and Fielding by choosing the middle-class for subject, at first confining themselves to Society and the County, but extending—with George Eliot —to all " Professions," and to a study of the poor. They made novels a reflection, and a criticism, of life.

It seems curious that, with the possible exception of Charlotte Brontë, women were all stern realists : while even her imaginativeness can scarcely be called romantic. The fact is, probably, that the heroes and heroines of romance were mainly conceived for young ladies, and popularly supposed to represent their ideal. Wherefore, when women began to express themselves, they—more or less consciously —set out to expose this fallacy: to prove that they could enjoy and face real life. No school of writers, indeed, has more fearlessly or more persistently created their characters from flesh and blood than the school represented by Jane Austen and George Eliot. None has dwelt more persistently on the trivial details of everyday life, the conquests of observation. Whether concerned, like Miss Burney, with the Comedy of Manners ; or, like George Eliot, with the Analysis of Soul ; they have one and all found their inspiration in human nature. And, in reality, this was the main progress achieved in fiction between Richardson and the nineteenth century—the growth on which the true modern novel was built up. Critics, indeed, have treated the " romance " and the " novel " as independent entities ; and if we limit the term romance to work preceding *Pamela*, we may accept their dictum. There is an essential difference between " making up " characters from a pseudo-ideal of the possibilities in human nature, and reflecting life. The old system, no doubt, was unhealthy in two ways : The ideals were not well-chosen, being composed by high-flown exaggeration ; and they were so mingled with actuality as to deceive the young person. For that matter the complaint is still living that girls and boys continually fancy real life will prove " just like a novel." It does not, of course, differ greatly from those of Jane Austen or George Eliot. The former, in fact, was accused-- in her own day—of setting too high a price on " prudence " in matrimony ; and the latter of encouraging a gloomy outlook.

Obviously realism, as here applied, has no connection with that Continental variety of the art which has more recently usurped the name. Women-writers, of this era, had not developed the cult of Ugliness, they did not confound painting with photography, they did not busy themselves with the morbid or the abnormal. Their works are not documents, but revelations. They dwell on manners, without ignoring their spiritual significance. To-day we have some use for the new realism, while dreading its predominance. They had none.

In enumerating the classes, or types, of humanity with whom the women-writers were mainly concerned, we were witnessing, of course, the allied progress of history. It was during the second half of the eighteenth, and the first of the nineteenth, centuries that the great English middle-class steadily grew in power and importance, boldly educating itself for influence,—before labour was heard in the land.

Fanny Burney has given us the "classes" at play; we fancy that Jane Austen, betraying their empty-mindedness, must have longed for, if she did not actually anticipate, better things ; Charlotte Brontë utters the first protest, indicating a struggle for existence ; George Eliot finds them busy about the meaning of life and its possibilities. Thus, finally, we read of real workers—men and women with the world at their feet, building an Empire, facing problems, questioning the gods.

And, in their own particular sphere,—the revelation of Woman,—we have seen already the same advance. Each of them gives us, for her own generation, a " new woman " ; creating, by the revelation of possibilities, an actual type. By teaching us what was " going on " *in women*, they taught women to be themselves. They opened the doors of Liberty towards Progress.

Minor achievements, on the other hand, were mostly directed towards the extension of subject matter, and the provision of new channels for fiction. Mrs. Radcliffe—who stood aside from the line of advance—established the School of Terror, applying romance methods to melodrama, with more power than we can find elsewhere in English. Maria Edgeworth introduced the story for children, which was not a tract, but the literary answer to " Tell me a story," the exploitation of nursery tales told by mothers from time immemorial. This was developed by Harriet Martineau and Charlotte Yonge, bearing fruit later in libraries of most varied achievement. As we all know, there have been several works of genius written expressly for children (as were not the *Pilgrim's Progress*, *Robinson Crusoe*, and *Gulliver's Travels*) ; innumerable delightful stories of a similar nature, and much inferior work.

The earlier women-writers set an excellent example in this field, if they retained overmuch moralising. They gave us a few nursery classics which show practical insight into the child's mind, and the gift of holding his interest by healthy wonder. We need only compare *Sandford and Merton* with *Frank* to recognise their peculiar fitness for such work.

The invention (by Mrs. Craik) of the " novel for the young person " is an allied achievement. It was developed by Charlotte Yonge, and has been always a legitimate province for women. Its dangers are over-sentimentalism (kin to Romance proper) and the idealism of the Woman's Man. Mrs. Craik gave us one type in *John Halifax, Gentleman*; there are two in Miss Yonge's *Heir of Redclyffe*.

It must be noted further that Harriet Martineau exploited philanthropy, and introduced the didactic element developed by George Eliot. Most women are born preachers—even Jane Austen occasionally points a moral—and this characteristic became prevalent early in their work. It was employed sometimes in the defence, or the exposure, of particular religious tenets; at others, on questions of pure ethics. There is a sense, of course, in which every story of life must carry its own moral; but George Eliot and most of the minor novelists obtrude this matter. In many cases the lesson is the motive, which is false art. However, the " novel with a purpose " clearly has come to stay. It outlived the period with which we are concerned, and is still vital. Speaking generally, the earlier women novelists contented themselves with raising the standard of domestic morality, upholding the family, and hinting at *one* ideal for the *two* sexes. George Eliot, indeed, went into individual cases with much detail ; but we note in all that their pet abomination is hypocrisy and cant.

Finally, and most important of all in outside influence, Maria Edgeworth invented the "national" novel—developed by Susan Ferrier and Mrs. Oliphant. We have noted already that in banishing the stage Irishman Miss Edgeworth inspired *Waverley* ; and the list of more recent examples (sprung from India, the " kailyard," the moorlands, and a hundred localities) would prove too formidable for passing enumeration. Her instinctive patriotism has sprung a mine that is practically inexhaustible and has given us much of our best work. The " Hardy " country and all " local colour " are similarly inspired. It is not too much to say that in this matter Miss Edgeworth introduced an entirely new element, only second in importance to the revelation of femininity, which is woman's chief contribution to the progress of Fiction.

While women were thus developing English fiction, with no rival of genius except Scott in his magnificent isolation, men had in some way advanced from Richardson to Thackeray and Dickens. It is worth noticing how far the two Victorian novelists showed the influence of feminine work, in what respects they reverted to the eighteenth century, and what new elements they introduced.

Both are still middle-class and, in one sense, domestic realists. Thackeray satirises Society (like Miss Burney and Jane Austen) ; Dickens works on manners, expounds causes, and takes up the poor. Both caught an enthusiasm for history from Scott, in which women did nothing of the first importance. Thackeray capped Lady Susan with Barry Lyndon, and Dickens produced a few overwrought washes of childhood—which women, curiously enough, never treated in their regular novels.

A certain resemblance in scope and arrangement has been noted already between *Vanity Fair* and *Evelina* ; but, speaking generally, it is obvious that Thackeray writes of Society more as a man of the world, and with broader insight, than either Miss Burney or Miss Austen. He not only observes, but criticises. One might say that, like all moderns, he feels morally responsible for the world. The " manners " which constitute the humour of

Dickens are more varied and, on the other hand, more caricatured than those of the women-writers. His fury against social evils is more public-spirited and less specialised ; his knowledge of the poor more intimate and genuinely sympathetic.

They have learnt, it would seem, from women to elaborate details in observation, to depend on truthful pictures of everyday life ; avoiding romance-characterisation or the aid of adventure in the composition of their plots. In fact, the development from Richardson's revolution is consecutive, taken up by the Victorians where the women left it. New side-issues are introduced ; the novel becomes more complex with the increased activities of civilisation, and grows with the growth of the middle classes. It is now the mouthpiece of what Commerce and Education began to feel and express. But the *direction* of progress is not changed.

So far it may fairly be said that Thackeray and Dickens have followed the women's lead, and bear witness to their influence.

Yet Thackeray reverts, particularly in *Pendennis*, to the " wild-oats " plot of Fielding ; Dickens is quite innocent of artistic construction, as perfected in Jane Austen ; and neither of them seems to have benefited at all from the extraordinary revelation of womanhood which we have traced from its earliest source.

Thackeray's heroines are, one and all, obviously made by a man for men. Amelia is a hearth-rug, with a pattern of pretty flowers. Beatrice and Blanche are variants of the eternal flirt—as man reads her. Lady Castlewood, Helen and Laura Pendennis are of the women who spend their lives waiting for the right man. Ethel Newcome is a man's dream ; and we venture to fancy that if ever a woman be born with genius to draw Becky Sharpe, she would find *something* to add to the picture.

The case of Dickens is even more desperate. His " pretty housemaids," indeed, are " done to a turn " ; and Nancy is of the immortals. He could illustrate with melodramatic intensity certain feminine characteristics, good or evil, tragic or comic. But all his heroines belong to a few obvious waxwork types—the idiotic " pet " or the fireside " angel " ; the " comfort " or the prig, composed of curls, blushes, and giggles ; looks of reproach and tender advice. Possibly Dora is rather more aggravating than Dolly Varden, Agnes is wiser than Kate Nickleby, but they all work by machinery, with visible springs.

It was reserved for George Meredith to understand women

APPENDIX

LIST OF MINOR WRITERS

(Their dates will indicate their place in our history of development : where they are not alluded to.)

MARGARET, DUCHESS OF NEWCASTLE (1624–1673), in her *CCXI Sociable Letters* (1664), tells an imaginary narrative by correspondence, which she describes as " rather scenes than letters, for I have endeavoured under cover of letters to express the humours of mankind." Also author of *Nature's Pictures drawn by Fancie's pencil* (1656).

FRANCES SHERIDAN.—Her *Memoirs of Miss Sydney Biddulph, extracted from her own Journal* (1761), made a name by its supreme melancholy. The heroine suffers from obeying her mother, and receives no reward. Dr. Johnson " did not know whether she had a right, on moral principles, to make her readers suffer so much."

MISS CLARA REEVE (1725–1803) began to write novels at fifty-one, and attempted in *The Old English Baron* (1777) to compromise with the School of Terror, by limiting herself to " the utmost *verge* of probability." Her " groan " is not interesting, and Scott complains of " a certain creeping and low line of narrative and sentiment " ; adding, however, that perhaps " to be somewhat *prosy* is a secret mode of securing a certain necessary degree of credulity from the hearers of a ghost-story."

ANNA SEWARD (1747–1809), a florid and picturesque poetess, whose verse-novel *Louisa* was valued in her day. She has a place in Scott's *Lives of the Novelists*.

CHARLOTTE SMITH (1749 – 1806). — Her *The Old Manor House* reveals independent. and novel, appreciation of scenery, illustrated by an unobtrusive familiarity with natural history. Her plots " bear the appearance of having been hastily run up," but her characterisation is vigorous. There is a " tone of melancholy " throughout.

HARRIET (1766–1851) and SOPHIA (1750–1824) LEE wrote some of the earliest historical novels—*The Recess; or, A Tale of other Times* (1783), introducing Queen Elizabeth and the " coarse virulence that marks her manners," and the *Canterbury Tales*, from which Byron borrowed.

MRS. BENNET, whose *Anna ; or, The Memoirs of a Welsh Heiress* (1785) is a bad imitation of Miss Burney, " with a catchpenny interspersion."

REGINA MARIA ROCHE, author of the once popular *The Children of the Abbey* (1798). Richardson, diluted with Mackenzie—in " elegant " language.

MRS. OPIE (1769–1853).—One of her best stories, *Adeline Mowbray; or, The Mother and Daughter* (1804), is partially founded on the life of Godwin, and shows the influence of his theories.

JANE PORTER (1776–1850), author of *Thaddeus of Warsaw* and *The Scottish Chiefs*, who claimed unjustly to have "invented" the historical romance, *copied* by Scott. Very famous in her day.

Also ANNA MARIA PORTER (1780–1832), author of *Don Sebastian*.

MRS. BRUNTON (1778–1818), author of the excellent *Self-Control* (1811) and *Discipline* (1814), which were overshadowed by Susan Ferrier. Lacking humour, her morality becomes tiresome, but she could draw living characters. The Highland experiences of her heroine, who, after marrying a minister, retained "a little of her coquettish sauciness," are significant for their date.

LADY MORGAN (1783–1859), as Miss Sydney Owenson, published *Wild Irish Girl* (1806), which is a fairly spirited réchauffé of all things Celtic. Thackeray found here the name Glorvina, meaning "sweet voice."

HENRIETTA MOSSE (otherwise Rouvière), whose *A Peep at our Ancestors* (1807) and other novels have been described as "blocks of spiritless and commonplace historic narrative."

ANNA ELIZABETH BRAY (1789–1883), author of *The Protestant*, various competent historical romances, and "local novels."

MRS. SHERWOOD, an evangelical propagandist, who naïvely enforced her views in *The Fairchild Family* (1818) and *Little Henry and his Bearer*.

ELIZABETH SEWELL 'set the style of High-Church propaganda, developed by Miss Yonge. Her chief tales, *Gertrude* and *Amy Herbert* (1844), are rigidly confined to everyday life. The characters, if living, are uninteresting ; and her morals are obtrusive.

CATHERINE GORE (1799–1861), author of over seventy tales ; and, in her own day, " the leader in the novel of fashion."

LADY G. FULLERTON (1812–1885), author of *Emma Middleton*, who shares with Miss Sewell the beginnings of High Church propaganda in fiction.

ANNE CALDWELL (MRS. MARSH), one of the best writers of the " revival " in domesticity. Her *Emilia Wyndham* (1846) was unfairly described as the " book where the woman breaks her desk open with her head." Though contemporary with *Pendennis*, has no ease in style.

MRS. ARCHER CLIVE (1801–1873), author of an early and well-told story of crime, entitled *Paul Ferroll* (1855).

MRS. HENRY WOOD (1814–1887).—A good plot-maker, whose *East Lynne*—both as book and play—has been phenomenally popular for many years ; though *The Channings*, and others, are better literature.

INDEX OF AUTHORS AND TITLES

I HAVE to thank the editor and publisher of
The Athenæum for permission to reprint the
chapter on "Parallel Passages"; the editor
and publisher of *The Gownsman* for permission to use "A Study in Fine Art";
Professor Gollancz and Messrs. Chatto &
Windus for permission to reprint the
section on "Cranford" which was written for
an Introduction to a reprint of that novel
in "The King's Classics."

A + S/